THE SCHOOL ENGINEER

ADAM ANDERSON

OF PERTH AND ST ANDREWS

1780-1846

Second edition, revised and enlarged

BY KENNETH J CAMERON

Number 47

Dundee

2007

ISBN 0 900019 44 1

Printed by Tayport Printers (Ltd)
Tel: (01382) 552381

CONTENTS

LIST OF ILLUSTRATIONS

Front Cover: The Fergusson Gallery (formerly Perth Waterworks) with inset portrait of Adam Anderson. Courtesy of Perth Museum and St Andrews University Museum Collections respectively.

Rear Cover: Detail of a Steam Engine for use in the Perth Waterworks, prepared by the Dundee Foundry, 1830. Courtesy of Dundee Central Library, Local History Centre.

Inside plates:

PREFACE TO THE FIRST EDITION

All historical research incurs debts and this work is no exception. The staffs of the National Library of Scotland, the Scottish Record Office and the Registrar-General for Scotland were, as always, unstintingly courteous and helpful. Acknowledgement is due also to my former 'base camp', Dundee University Library, for furnishing most of the bibliographical aids and interlibrary loan facilities so essential to any research. Generous assistance was provided by many, including Mr J.V. Howard, New College Library, Edinburgh; Mrs Couperwhite and staff at Greenock Public Library; Mr W.H. Rutherford, former Executive Secretary of the Royal Society of Edinburgh; Mr W.E. Wolsey, Kincardine-on-Forth; Dr Hine, Department of Humanity, University of St Andrews; Mr N. McCorkindale, former Rector of Perth Academy; and Mr J.A. Bryce, Sandeman Public Library, Perth. Among friends and colleagues who suggested sources, furnished advice, saved me from impetuous judgements, and invariably offered encouragement were Mr R.N. Smart, Keeper of Muniments, University of St Andrews; Mr S. Connolly, District Archivist, Perth; and Dr L.A. Williams, Department of Modern History, University of Dundee. All the above, needless to say, are absolved from any blame for remaining sins of omission or commission. To Dr W. Findlay, Perth, I am indebted for several of the illustrations deployed in this publication; also, to St Andrews University for giving permission to reproduce Anderson's portrait.

Tribute must be paid also to Mr Fred Anderson, Ontario, Canada, great-grandson of Adam Anderson, for constant interest, help and encouragement. His enthusiastic garnering of family archives was an essential foundation for this publication and a stirring example to others. Acknowledgement is readily made, additionally, to the Carnegie Trust for the Universities of Scotland for travel and subsistence grants that greatly facilitated the research. To all the above, I readily record my unqualified appreciation. Particular thanks are due, however, to Dr Chris Whatley, editor of the Abertay Historical Society, and to his predecessor, Dr Annette M. Smith, for reading previous drafts of the text and suggesting many improvements. Finally, but certainly not least, gratitude (and sympathy) are due to my wife, Sheila, and to my children, Neil, Eilidh and Iseabail, for sharing their lives too with Adam Anderson and, above all, putting up with the knowledge that he is unlikely to be the last intruder in their home.

Kenneth J. Cameron, University of Strathclyde, June 1987.

PREFACE TO THE SECOND EDITION

Debts incurred in 1988 remain undiminished with time, and appreciation to all who contributed to the first edition is warmly recorded anew, tinged with regret only by the knowledge that in some cases it is sadly now posthumous. This revised, extended edition draws heavily on the emergence of a significant new collection of correspondence, principally from Adam Anderson to his parents. The letters covered Anderson's later years as a student and his early career as a family tutor. These fleshed out fortuitously the formative period of his life, which was least adequately informed by available sources when the previous edition was written. Personal correspondence is typically a source that offers clearer insights than public records into character and motivation. The Anderson letters were no exception; and a more rounded view of the subject is hopefully the outcome.

Inevitably, with an augmented edition, new debts were incurred. The possibility of a revision (rather than a corrected reprint) owes most initially to Mr Patrick Nicholson of Dublin, a direct descendant of Adam Anderson, who first drew the author's attention to the deposit of the new accession of Anderson correspondence in the University of St Andrews Library (ms38329/1-52). His enthusiasm and generosity in furnishing additional family background, constant encouragement and, not least, thought-provoking questions over several years have also been much appreciated. To Mr Nicholson, and to his cousin, Mrs Lucy Kavanagh of Limerick, warm thanks are due too for supplying images and giving permission to reproduce them. Complementary appreciation is gladly expressed likewise to Dr Norman Reid, Keeper of Manuscripts, University of St Andrews Library, for kindly granting permission to quote extensively from the University's augmented Anderson deposit, and to his staff for helpful assistance during visits to the Library's Special Collections.

For permission to reproduce additional images used in this edition, gratitude is recorded to St Andrews University; Dundee Central Library, Local History Centre; Perth Museum; and Perth &

Kinross Archives. Mr Steve Connelly, wearing twin hats, as Archivist to Perth & Kinross Council and as President of the Abertay Historical Society, gave unstinting practical support throughout the preparation of this edition from inception to completion. This edition has greatly benefited from his identification and sourcing of suitable images, and the author is also indebted to him for drawing his attention to Anderson's consultant report on Auchterarder's water system. The Society's General Secretary, Mr Matthew Jarron, was an energetic and instantaneous source of helpful advice on publishing in general, and on the digital technicalities and copyright practicalities of images in particular. Likewise, tribute must also be paid to Dr Billy Kenefick, joint book editor of the Society, whose editorial scalpel judiciously removed warts from the author's text and enhanced the final product enormously in the process.

The author, like the Society, has benefited greatly from the energy and enthusiasm of all three officebearers. Thanks are also due to the Council of the Abertay Historical Society for providing this opportunity to bring new material on Adam Anderson into the public domain. Needless to say, whilst the end product has been enormously improved through the advice of others, all residual shortcomings and inaccuracies remain the author's.

Finally, I gladly record once more the contribution of Sheila, my wife, whose encouragement and practical support have been unflagging: once again, her IT skills helped to remedy and, to a gratifying extent, camouflage the author's digital limitations. This edition is dedicated, with gratitude and love, jointly to her and to the memory of my parents, the late John and Kathleen Cameron; without the direct (and indirect) contributions of all three, neither edition would have seen the light of day.

Kenneth J Cameron, University of Strathclyde, January 2007

INTRODUCTION

In 1972, after energetic advocacy by the local Civic Trust, the former Perth Town Council embarked on the restoration of one of Scotland's outstanding examples of industrial archaeology. Two years later the so-called 'Round House', Perth's original waterworks overlooking the river Tay, was returned to most of its former splendour. The demolition of later accretions revealed the building as it first appeared in the 1830s, exhibiting to full visual effect its rotunda, cast iron dome, and columnar stone chimney capped with replica of the original urn. It was possible to appreciate again the lyrical description used by the *Perth Courier* in 1834 on its completion, when the journal spoke of the impressive sight awaiting paddle steamers on their arrival from Dundee:

> The water reservoir at once starting into full view, unencumbered by any other building and with its chaste and beautiful architecture, appears like a temple embosomed in a wood.[1]

Visitors were equally impressed. To the English bibliographer, Thomas Dibdin, contemplating them in 1837, the waterworks were:

> A lesson to learn - or a model to copy - for all England. Here was deformity converted into beauty, and a nuisance rendered a picturesque accessory.[2]

Yet their significance was more than aesthetic. Behind the architectural creation was an engineering triumph: the provision of the first effective supply of clean drinking water for the city of Perth. Even more remarkable, it was the single-handed achievement of an amateur engineer after professionals had failed. The designer was a schoolmaster, Adam Anderson, then rector of the local academy.

Had this been his sole essay in applied science, Anderson's claim to a footnote in the history of technology would still have been secure, but it was merely the most visible of many. He previously furnished the town with its first gas supply, and he remained Perth's resident scientific consultant for fully a generation. His talents were devoted unstintingly to a range of public enterprises during that era of accelerating change. The adoption of uniform weights and measures, navigational improvements on the Tay, and the preservation of the town's environment - from irreparable damage at the hands of railway entrepreneurs and their municipal backers - were three legacies with scientific or engineering connotations. Clearly, he was a man of his time. After due allowance is made for undoubted ability and originality, it required the limitations of scientific knowledge, and the intense local self-sufficiency of early nineteenth-century society, to permit such a widespread innovatory influence by one individual.

The same localism and self-reliance stimulated demands for Anderson to deploy his considerable moral influence on the side of political and social stability in Perth during the turmoil of the reform period. He responded with characteristic energy, attempting to alleviate social distress, promoting working-class education as an alternative outlet for radical aspirations, and channelling popular protest into constitutional politics. His significance here was less what he accomplished, which is more difficult to measure, and rather what he represented. In the aftermath of the Great Reform Act of 1832, as well as during its passage, he personified the enhanced role of the middle-classes in political life. If leadership was the new norm for this stratum of society in most urban constituencies, and common for certain specific professional groups within it, this torch was less usual in the hands of a schoolteacher.

Forsaking his original clerical aspirations, it was in the combined roles of teacher and scientist that Anderson first and foremost saw himself. As such he was, particularly by contemporary standards, an outstanding success as a communicator, establishing a good rapport with pupils and students alike. It was his academic ability that inspired the gifted, but if he had a weakness at school level it was that he left some of the less able bemused. On the other hand, it led to a respectable output of scientific papers, recognition in terms of academic honours, and eventually the realisation of his life-long ambition for a university chair at St Andrews. At the time such an appointment was the pinnacle of Scottish science. Apart from a handful of years as a family tutor in Edinburgh, Anderson attained it though spending his entire career in Tayside, almost all in one relatively small provincial town. In the twenty-first century such an achievement, following thirty years' school teaching, would be unthinkable; but in the vibrant state of provincial and amateur science at Queen Victoria's accession, when the distinction between secondary and tertiary education was ill defined, and before later centrifugal forces emerged, it was possible.

What was the taproot of an energy, which could stimulate such a multiplicity of activities - scientific, engineering, educational and political? From a firm belief in Christianity's capacity in the moral sphere, and in the complementary role of science in the material, to transform the quality of life, the theme of reconciliation runs through his diverse activities. He attempted, and from aptitude and early experience, was peculiarly well-equipped, to bridge gulfs between religion and science, pure and applied science, academic and popular science, amateurism and professionalism, and not least the conflicting aspirations of different groups in society. From physics into politics he carried a vision of scientific symmetry, balance and order. Fused with a love of humanity in general, an intense civic pride in his adopted town in particular, and legitimate aspiration for personal fulfillment and advancement, this released a veritable stream of creativity. As scientific specialisation advanced and localism retreated, Da Vinci type polymaths were soon to become an extinct species — but not before some of them, including Adam Anderson, left an enduring imprint.

NOTES

[1]   *Perth Courier*, 17 July, 1834.

[2]   Quoted in R. Lamont-Brown and P. Adamson, *Victorian and Edwardian Perthshire from rare photographs*, (St Andrews: Alvie Publications, 1985), 9.

1

ST ANDREWS – FIRST ENCOUNTER

Unlike some of its more easterly neighbours on the Fife coast, Kincardine-on-Forth survived the economic dislocations of eighteenth-century Scotland in tolerably good shape. *The First Statistical Account* could report a 'pretty large village ... containing 312 houses, substantially built' and even boasting the status symbol of its own post office. True, by the 1790s, the formerly prosperous coal industry and saltpans had faded into history, but shipping at least remained. The sloops and brigantines that once exported coal and carried salt to Leith judiciously switched allegiance to new opportunities in nearby ports. Indeed, the opening of the Carron ironworks, followed by the advent of the Forth and Clyde Canal, had ensured a continuing, even an expanding role for local shipping, with tentacles reaching the Mediterranean, the Levant and Scandinavia, in addition to coasting activities. Despite diversifying interests, however, most ship owners remained domiciled in Kincardine – at this time still an outlying part of historic Perthshire on the Forth estuary - leaving mute testimony to their numbers and prosperity in fine examples of funerary sculpture in Tulliallan churchyard. Their resilience and adaptability maintained a viable shipbuilding industry too, as they took full advantage of a good roadstead and a hard gravel beach, to construct and launch numerous sloops and brigantines. From a handful of ships at the nadir of its fortunes, the Kincardine fleet had expanded by 1795 to seventy-five vessels, amounting to 4,043 tons and employing three hundred sailors. These entrepreneurial activities contributed to a near doubling of the population between 1755 and 1793.[1] Kincardine's geographical location, close to the once vibrant, but now decayed east coast ports of Scotland's trading past, yet firmly on the edges of her industrial future, was the key to the community's economic buoyancy and outlook.

The most prominent local landowner, Archibald Cochrane, ninth Earl of Dundonald, personified the transitional nature of the time and place. Representing a social order rooted in the past, like many landowning contemporaries in the Industrial Revolution, he was anxious to exploit new opportunities to strengthen its economic foundations. In his case the outcome was a disaster: pursuing unprofitable, scientific enthusiasms, he bankrupted his estates. But his experiments with the illuminating powers of coal gas demonstrated an impressive, if economically suicidal dedication to find a practical application for pure scientific theory.[2] Whether aware of his activities or not, enquiring young minds in the locality were undoubtedly influenced by the intellectual ferment associated with the Enlightenment which underpinned this climate of investigation. Perhaps it was not surprising that one of these young local contemporaries should subsequently become a successful applied scientist in general, and promote the gas industry in particular.

Adam Anderson was born in Tulliallan parish on 29 June 1780, and third of four identifiable sons of a Kincardine shipmaster, Andrew Anderson. At the time of her marriage, his mother, Ann Moon, came from Errol in the Carse of Gowrie, and was probably daughter of the tenant at the Mill of Errol. Besides two surviving younger sisters, he had, through an earlier marriage by his father, an older half-sister, Janet, born in 1766. A close relationship with her reputedly brought pecuniary advantages to Adam after she married prosperous Culross ship owner, Charles Jamieson, in 1789. If true, this may have contributed to the quality of his subsequent education, since no surviving evidence points to undue affluence in his father's economic and social circumstances,[3] despite the latter's subtle elevation in status from 'shipmaster' to 'ship owner' in family correspondence from the end of 1803. That correspondence, combined with parish records and family gravestones, confirm the family's continued residence in Kincardine, but Anderson's early life and specific formative influences may only be conjectured. Whether, for example, he was educated at the local parish school with its notoriously high fees, or in either of two local private adventure schools, or elsewhere, is uncertain.[4]

In 1797, Anderson arrived at St Andrews to attend United College, where he would remain for the next three years. In going to university Anderson was the exception within his family. His two surviving brothers, John and Andrew, and other immediate relations, continued to pursue the family's shipping interests in both coastal and international waters. Anderson nonetheless carried into his student years, and later life, a technical knowledge of ships and their construction, and a familiarity with commerce and meteorological conditions, acquired originally in Kincardine and refreshed through continuing close family and maritime contacts. He was thus a frequent visitor to harbours and an avid reader of newspaper columns relating to international affairs and shipping , partly to keep track of his relatives' movements and their commercial prospects. It was a utilitarian aspect of his 'education' that would help him more easily to straddle the divide between academe and society in general.

Aged seventeen on initial matriculation, Anderson was comparatively mature compared with many of his contemporaries in the Scottish university system. He also arrived at St Andrews academically well-prepared. At the outset he matriculated in the junior Greek literature class, but concurrent attendance at the senior rather than junior Latin class, though not unknown, was unusual and implies a thorough classical grounding in the course of his pre-university schooling. His first two sessions were devoted to the initial stages of the traditional arts course, but it was during Anderson's third year that his academic ability was clearly demonstrated. Encompassing in one session senior Greek, Latin, ethics, natural philosophy and mathematics, he effectively telescoped the last two years of the arts curriculum into one. Two further years at St Andrews were then spent in Divinity Hall.[5]

Anderson's curricular progress was mirrored in his use of the university library; a facility benefiting from legal deposit, this was justly admired for its store of books in all sciences and was accessible to every student for a small annual payment. He was charged (like his contemporary, Thomas Chalmers, and two-thirds of students) at the lowest, or 'ternar' rate, tending to confirm a family background that was not deemed comparatively affluent, though it was by no means a pointer to poverty. Nearly ninety loans under his name in the library's extant borrowing registers reflect the overall evolution of his studies: history, geography and *belles-lettres* in the early years, supplanted firstly by science, then by theology. Catholicity of interest was mirrored in microcosm in intermittent loans of *Encyclopaedia Britannica* and Sinclair's *Statistical Account*.[6] In Anderson's case recorded loans probably did genuinely reflect a conscientious attitude to study. In March 1802, reporting to his parents retrospectively that he had been unwell, he attributed his ill health to sitting up too late at his studies. He had 'often sat to 5 in the morning, which produced a headach [sic] next day and at last terminated in a great spitting, & want of appetite.'[7] If a hardworking image was no doubt emphasised to elicit parental sympathy and approval, there is no reason to doubt that Anderson was industrious as well as able.

Despite his bout of ill health however, St Andrews, with its population of 2,700 and coastal location, enjoyed an enviable reputation for pure air, clean water and freedom from epidemic disease. During his sojourn the town was to suffer nonetheless, like the rest of Britain, from the general economic dislocation caused by continual warfare with revolutionary France. Within three years of Anderson's arrival students were to face spiralling prices for basic necessities, notably coal, bread and beef. Soon he would recount to his parents that people in the town were stealing through absolute necessity and that a student had been expelled from College for swindling a peck of meal. Anderson personally had the consolation however, of constant moral and material support from his family. The carrier and the post brought laundry and news from home during term, and he resided for long periods during the extended summer vacations with his comparatively well-to-do uncle, John Moon, whose property of Balgonie lay on the flat carse land between Abernethy and Newburgh, close to Mugdrum island on the river Tay. There he fared upon 'dainties such as Lamb & Cabbage, Salmon, Gooseberry-pies, etc', as well as having access to his horses and to the private library of another relative.[8] In addition, Anderson was well placed to supplement his pecuniary resources. He turned his wide range of academic study to personal profit by undertaking extensive paid tutoring. Clearly an established practice by 1800, he lamented in

November that:

> There are few gentlemen's sons at College
> this session, which has rendred [sic] the
> procuring pupils a matter of very
> considerable difficulty; however I have
> been offer'd, till I have rejected them. I read
> Greek & Latin 2 hours a day with a
> Gentleman's son of the name of Hunter,
> who has an estate at Blackness; for whom I
> receive 5 Guineas. I also read Mathematics
> with another, 1 hour for which I receive $2\frac{1}{2}$
> Guineas. – Lastly, I teach Writing &
> Arithmetic to a nephew and a niece of Dr
> Rotheram one of the Professors at $\frac{1}{2}$
> Guinea per month. I had an offer of
> another, but whom I have not accepted of,
> as thinking it might interrupt my own
> studies.

These commitments, doubtless a factor exacerbating his own need for late night study, were undertaken to meet the costs of essentials, above all bread and coal, but there were other requirements: 'if my finances would permit, I would have a big coat, as I have to go out to the boys at night'.[9] Of significance for the future, these tutoring engagements gave Anderson a first taste of teaching; and although the direction of his career demonstrated ambivalence for several years, he would remain in a teaching role of some kind throughout the rest of his life.

With fewer than two hundred alumni, two-thirds at United College, St Andrews University was a very close society. Each student was personally known to the staff, so 'innocent amusements' could be safely regulated, ensuring good behaviour, whilst competition and application were encouraged by annual public examinations in the university hall. Opportunities abounded for able and ambitious students to impress academic mentors and cultivate useful patrons for the future. In his fifth year Anderson was gratified to be invited for the first time to have supper at the home of Principal James Playfair, Principal of United College, and to have tea with Lady Montcrieffe [sic],[10] both prospectively useful contacts in the longer-term. Likewise, students were familiar to their fellows, but in that privileged milieu, pitfalls could entrap the socially mobile from less affluent backgrounds, where they felt insecure. During an after dinner walk, Anderson was embarrassed in front of other students, when greeted on familiar terms by an indigent family acquaintance, whose 'appearance did not say a great deal for his quality'. He had appeared, 'if not a near relation to be at least an intimate acquaintance.' Following teasing by his companions, Anderson taxed his parents to be more discreet in divulging details about him to others.[11] It was not the last occasion on which Anderson became protective over his social status and concerned about potential damage to his reputation from failing to conform to contemporaries' expectations.

Anderson valued social relationships and his interpersonal skills became well-honed, but that did not imply dependence on the company of others. Left behind at St Andrews by all his companions when Divinity College rose in April 1801, he felt 'a little dejected … but time makes one suit himself to any situation … I am as happy in my solitary state as formerly when surrounded with comrades.'[12] In due course that self-reliance and self-confidence would equip him to forge ahead with innovative public projects and to withstand critics. Among Anderson's contemporaries and friends, the dominant personality was the future church leader from Anstruther, Thomas Chalmers (1780-1847), whose attendance at Divinity Hall overlapped with his own sojourn at United College. Despite a reputation for a fluctuating temperament, Chalmers was popular with his fellow students who tolerated his whimsical withdrawals into meditation on abstract ideas.[13] In this period, prior to Chalmers' evangelical conversion, a lifelong friendship began. Anderson later recalled 'the days of thoughtlessness & folly', when Chalmers ridiculed 'the doctrines of Scripture with regard to the necessity of Regeneration.' The former had 'occasionally joined in the laugh … rather from sympathy, than because I thought them fit subjects for being treated with levity or contempt', but he consoled himself in retrospect that both had changed for the better.[14] Anderson observed, however, that 'at one period no two individuals could be more intimately acquainted.'[15] The friendship was natural, based on similar backgrounds in small east coast communities and shared interests in divinity and science. Ironically, it was only after their deaths that the link became complete and familial, when Anderson's nephew, Charles Jamieson, married Chalmers' niece, Grace, in 1851.

Chalmers left St Mary's College in 1799. A year later, having completed his arts course at United College, Anderson in turn transferred to Divinity College. Towards the close of his first session, in April 1801, he then undertook the trouble and cost, albeit probably at his uncle's expense, of graduating MA, a precondition for an application for an Exchequer Divinity grant, and the usual motivation for the investment. A month later he proceeded to apply for a King's Bursary in Divinity.[16] The bursary was neither certain nor immediate, but Anderson had another potential monetary iron in the fire. A vacancy in the perennial post of assistant to the ailing professor of mathematics, Nicholas Vilant, had occurred again by the end of December 1801. Confident that there were only two candidates in the running, Anderson boasted privately that he was inferior to his rival 'in no branch of mathematics'. His confidence had been boosted by a challenge from Vilant to the two aspirants to demonstrate two difficult propositions: only Anderson had accepted the test, successfully demonstrating both.[17] As late as April 1802, however, Vilant had still not declared his choice for the vacancy. By that date, having sworn allegiance to the sovereign (George III), abjured the Jacobite 'pretender' (Prince Henry Benedict, Cardinal Duke of York), and paid the requisite fee of half a guinea, Anderson had fulfilled all necessary conditions of the bursary. Although no grant would be received until the end of the session, securing the mathematics assistantship now seemed a lower priority, since the emolument attached to the post amounted to only £40 and would require the surrender of the bursary (of £30). Moreover, it would preclude him accepting a possible invitation, which he now anticipated, of appointment as a family tutor, a common source of funding for part-time theological studies. If the mathematics post were offered, Anderson admitted to his parents, he did not know what to do.[18]

At the end of July, whilst encamped again for the summer vacation at Balgonie, Anderson spent some days at St Andrews, receiving warm hospitality from the professoriate. Concurrently, he learned that he would be given first offer of a family tutorship to two boys expected from England.[19] Whether this was the engagement finally accepted is unknown, but in October 1802 the university senate heard of Anderson's intention 'to reside elsewhere during the ensuing session'; this led to the prompt termination of his bursary.[20] A month later, Anderson had re-located to Edinburgh, having accepted a post as family tutor to an Angus family, the Greenhills of Fern.

NOTES

[1]   D. Berridge, *Culross and Tulliallan, or Perthshire on Forth*, (Edinburgh: Blackwood, 1885), 226-7; O[ld] S[tatistical] A[ccount] *of Scotland]*, rev. ed., (Wakefield: EP Publishing, 1976), vol. xi, parish of Tulliallan, 616-23; J. F. Erskine, *General view of the agriculture of the county of Clackmannan; and some of the adjacent parishes, situated in the counties of Perth and Stirling*, (Edinburgh: Printed by H. Inglis, 1795), 14-15.

[2]   D. Berridge, *op. cit.*, 232-8.

[3]   [Edinburgh:] HM General Register Office for Scotland], OPR 397/1 Tulliallan parish, register of births; OPR 397/2, Tulliallan parish, register of marriages. The records of the Royal Society of Edinburgh (information kindly supplied by Mr W. H. Rutherford) and some other secondary sources cite 27 June 1783 as his date of birth. The latter's absence from the OPR, the timespan of siblings's birth dates, and Anderson's entry in the 1841 census reinforce the 1780 entry as the more likely date and discredit 1783. See too NAS. Census enumerators' books, CEN.1841/387 (Perth).

[4]   *OSA*, vol. xi, parish of Tulliallan, 625.

[5]   For information on his university career I am indebted to Mr R.N. Smart, former University Archivist, University of

St Andrews. See too *The matriculation roll of the University of St Andrews, 1747-1897;* ed. by J. Maitland Anderson, (Edinburgh: Blackwood, 1905), 45.

6   [St Andrews,]Univ[ersity of] St And[rews] Libr[ary], Spec[ial] Coll[ections]. University Library students' receipt books, 1795-1801.

7   Univ. St And. Libr., Spec. Coll., MS38329/7. A. Anderson to parents, St Andrews, 20 Mar. 1802.

8   *OSA*, vol. x, parishes of St Andrews and of St Leonards, 709-10, 717-23. Univ. St And. Libr., Spec. Coll., MS38329/2. A. Anderson to parents, Balgonie, 12 July 1800; MS38329/4. Same to same, St Andrews, 18 Apr. 1801.

9   Univ. St And. Libr., Spec. Coll., MS38329/3. Same to same, St Andrews, 15 Nov. 1800. This quotation and others from the Anderson correspondence are reproduced by kind permission of the Keeper of Manuscripts, University of St Andrews Library.

10   Univ. St And. Libr., Spec. Coll., MS38329/7. Same to same, St Andrews, 20 Mar. 1802.

11   Univ. St And. Libr., Spec. Coll., MS38329/5. Same to same, St Andrews, 6 Dec. 1801.

12   Univ. St And. Libr., Spec. Coll., MS38329/4. Same to same, St Andrews, 18 Apr. 1801.

13   S. J. Brown, *Thomas Chalmers and the godly commonwealth in Scotland*, (Oxford: Oxford U.P., 1982), 1-16.

14   Univ. St And. Libr., Spec. Coll., T[homas | C | halmers] L[etters], MS30385/1. A. Anderson to T. Chalmers, Perth, 19 Nov. 1818.

15   [Edinburgh:] N[ew] C[ollege] L[ibrary], T[homas] C[halmers | P[apers], CHA 4.7.1. Same to same, Perth, 24 Oct. 1818.

16   Univ. St And. Libr., Spec. Coll., MS38329/4. A. Anderson to parents, St Andrews, 18 Apr. 1801; UY 452/10. St And[rews] Sen[ate] Min[utes] 5 May 1801

17   Univ. St And. Libr., Spec. Coll., MS38329/5. A. Anderson to parents, St Andrews, 6 Dec. 1801.

18   Univ. St And. Libr., Spec. Coll., MS38329/7. Same to same, St Andrews, 20 Mar. 1802; UY 452/10. St And. Sen. Min., 8 Apr. 1802.

19   Univ. St And. Libr., Spec. Coll., MS38329/10. A. Anderson to parents, Balgonie, 30 July 1802.

20   Univ. St And. Libr., Spec. Coll., UY 452/10. St And. Sen. Min., 4 Oct. 1802. Paradoxically, as he departed, the vacant assistantship to the professor of mathematics would be filled in 1802-03 by the return of Thomas Chalmers to his original alma mater.

2

TO STICKIT MINISTER OR SCIENTIST?

Charles Greenhill, a man of humble parentage, schooled in law, rose to become factor to the earls of Southesk in Angus for upwards of forty years. His success was confirmed and publicly proclaimed in 1797 with the purchase of estates in Fern (or Fearn) parish. From 1802 for seven years Anderson was to lead a bipolar existence, spending most of the year as resident tutor with Greenhill's two (later three) sons in Edinburgh, where they attended school or university, but migrating annually in the second half of July or August to Angus for two or three months. Although the Greenhills were the leading heritors in Fern, the estate of Old Montrose, owned by Sir David Carnegie, was the principal residence of Anderson and the younger Greenhills on their yearly sojourn in the north. This estate was conveniently located on the south-western fringes of the tidal, land-locked Montrose Basin, a sporting paradise, especially for wild fowling, and accessible to the town of Montrose. The vacations were enlivened too with visits to the Greenhills' numerous relatives and friends amongst the county gentry, as well as to their small country house in the foothills of the Grampians. This annual retreat to Angus was generally pleasant and relaxing. Arriving at Old Montrose in August 1804, en route to the Grampians, Anderson looked forward eagerly to plenty of amusement - hunting, shooting and fishing - and to laying in a 'stock of health' for the ensuing winter.[1]

Edinburgh was nonetheless Anderson's main domicile for the next seven years, and it provided complementary stimulation. With 82,560 inhabitants, as enumerated in the 1801 census, it had recently expanded substantially and remained the largest city in Scotland, albeit shortly to lose that crown to Glasgow. But Edinburgh could offer more than economic success; it had also entered its 'golden age', luring visitors from near and far, and housing a resident community of leading philosophers, literati and thinkers. The values of the Scottish Enlightenment were nurtured within its bounds, whilst those of the past were challenged. The inauguration of the *Edinburgh Review* by a group of brilliant young Whigs in 1802, the year of Anderson's arrival, encapsulated the city's intellectual energy and impulse for new ideas. The following year, under the aegis of Robert Reid, and commencing with Heriot Row, Edinburgh would launch on a further major expansion that would create its 'second new town', clothing the north-facing steep slopes of the first, but with buildings of enhanced architectural quality. It was the old town however, decaying and now largely deserted by wealthy society, which provided the city's lodgings; like many others, Anderson experienced their variable quality.[2] During his first winter in the capital, a Mrs Mackenzie and family provided a comfortable berth, even plying him with salts and attention when he was stricken with ill-health, but her rooms ceased to be available after August 1804. Cunningham's Lodgings in South College Street then temporarily sufficed, though they were too crowded. Securing acceptable accommodation in Edinburgh proved more difficult than Anderson had anticipated. With nostalgia he recalled the intimacy of St Andrews, 'where one could be informed of the Characters of all the different people that let lodgings in the space of half an hour, here all that knowledge must be acquired by dear bought experience'. Anderson felt compelled to move, eventually finding accommodation that was 'agreeable enough' with a Mrs Preston in Nicholson Street, to whom he returned for the winter of 1805.[3] Deserting unsatisfactory lodgings proved easier than avoiding unwelcome guests. Recovering from influenza in April 1803, he was plagued with repeated visits from a family acquaintance, Mrs Hodge, 'attended by her train of famine looking sisters & her aid de champ [sic], Miss Donald'. As at St Andrews his parents took the brunt of Anderson's irritation, this time for divulging his address; his lodgings were not 'a levee for strangers'.[4] Two years later an indigent relative would complain of the reception he received during a visit to Edinburgh. Anderson responded that his relative could hardly have expected to 'walk the street arm in arm' with him: as a family tutor, he required 'to maintain a degree of respect in the eyes of the Greenhills family, which would be no ways increased by letting them know all my relations'.[5]

A brief sabbatical as family tutor was a normal means of funding part-time study on divinity courses. Thomas Chalmers had resumed his theological studies and Anderson's original intention was the same. Indeed, no hiatus was even planned; from the outset his initial salary from Greenhill was earmarked for class fees in Hebrew and church history, the two optional classes at Edinburgh University's Faculty of Divinity. Even this stressed still limited finances, since his uncle at Balgonie, who had suffered a paralytic stroke in the summer, had not responded to a plea for a loan. John Moon had allegedly gained an impression from an unrevealed source, that Anderson's lengthy residences with him had been motivated by long-term mercenary expectations. Anderson was frustrated that his father had not forwarded to him a copy of the original letter of accusation in this 'dark affair'. Betraying hurt youthful pride and indignation he consoled himself with the thought that he would soon 'be able to do for myself, when I shall not be dependent on the smiles or favours of any man'. Four months later he had still heard nothing from Balgonie, almost despairing 'of hearing again from that quarter'.[6]

Meantime, from the perspective of pursuing a clerical career, his choice of employer at least appeared judicious. In November 1802, a mere two months after Anderson's appointment, John Gillanders, minister of Fern parish, died. Greenhill, as principal heritor of the parish, attempted to persuade the Presbytery of Brechin to reserve the resulting vacancy for his tutor, a proposal that fell foul of Assembly law. With persistence, however, he then endeavoured to have the church living 'transferred' temporarily to another family tutor, who was capable of accepting it, but with an obligation to surrender the charge to Anderson, when the latter was ready. Greenhill had in fact refused to listen to several applications for the vacancy until he had ascertained whether it would be possible for Anderson to accept, besides securing the interest of Sir David Carnegie, 'a matter of no small consequence', on his tutor's behalf.

Even with such influence, however, these stratagems proved unsuccessful. Six months later, following a royal presentation of David Harris for the Fern vacancy, the Presbytery obtained written assurance of Greenhill's 'full concurrence' in the presentation. Despite the outcome, Anderson was pleased that Greenhill was 'so warmly disposed to assist me in my future views', especially a mere two months after assuming responsibility for his sons. Moreover, during his residence in Angus, Anderson also became acquainted through the Greenhills with a great part of the gentry of the district, which he hoped would be 'nothing to my disadvantage'.[7] His energies were accordingly thrown anew into theological studies, the session at Edinburgh closing on 18 April 1803. Anderson had earlier presented a discourse on the text: 'By these words learn of me'. Having shown it to 'Dr Hunter' – presumably Andrew Hunter, professor of divinity - who 'was never very high in his encomiums', he had been gratified to receive as much praise as he could expect.[8]

Despite Anderson's apparent dedication to a clerical calling, others at least envisaged, even at this point, that he might be induced to follow an alternative career. Within six months of commencing his tutorship, he was approached to consider the rectorship of the recently founded and well-endowed academy at Inverness, a post that carried emoluments of £200 per year. This was declined, since his present situation prevented him 'from accepting any offer of this nature, even supposing I were willing to do so'. He had no doubt that a former St Andrews contemporary, Alexander Nimmo, who had taught at Fortrose Academy since 1802, would be appointed. The prediction proved correct: two years later Nimmo secured the post, and with active assistance from Anderson, who examined him in a mock interview, anticipating 'almost the very identical questions' in Greek, Latin, French, mathematics, natural philosophy, and chemistry, which were later posed by the interviewing board of Edinburgh professors.[9] Inverness was not the only temptation. In late 1803, an acquaintance of the Greenhills broached an offer with a similar salary to enter on board a ship as tutor to an admiral's sons. Anderson rejected this too, on the grounds that his parents would have been averse to his accepting anything of the kind before the completion of his studies.[10]

Anderson's time was directed meantime at a range of activities, as well as religious studies. The prime claim was made, of course, by his two charges. The older Greenhill pupil, Alexander, was doing well, but Anderson had to admit that his younger pupil James was 'a hard block to work upon'. To 'shape him into any sort of figure like a scholar', he asserted, 'I must lay my account with many chisels of patience.' Although circumscribed by guardian and tutorial obligations, Anderson still had freedom to follow his own pursuits. An Adam Anderson had been admitted to membership of Edinburgh Subscription Library, a dining-cum-book club, in 1800, and retained that status until at least 1808.[11] With this probable exception, Anderson appears to have left no overt footprints in the city's societies. His interests, constrained by guardianship responsibilities, were more individualistic, ranging from angling to education. In spring 1803, he decided to attend a course in the new scientific discipline of chemistry, a subject that had given rise to one of the eight new chairs founded within the Faculty of Medicine at Edinburgh between 1720 and 1770.[12] In the wake of Lavoisier, this dynamic discipline was, in Anderson's eyes, 'now an essential part of the Education of a Scholar'. Botany, 'a very agreeable & useful study', fell into the same definition, as did the natural history class, taught during the summer. Although the fees for attendance were high, Anderson did 'not wish to be ignorant of any one branch of science when I have an opportunity of procuring it.'[13] He brought to study an investigative approach that could be risky: in October 1803, a chemical experiment exploded, showering his face with glass splinters, whilst ladies in the room were put 'in the greatest alarm'. He vowed to be more careful in the future.[14]

This diverse, experimental impulse would nonetheless later provide the catalyst for projects that drew on an impressive range of scientific disciplines and engineering skills. Indeed, early interest in practical applications was already apparent and catholic. At St Andrews and Edinburgh, his correspondence included a torrent of advice to his parents, for instance, on their medical ailments, and the carrier regularly conveyed therapies from medication to leeches to Kincardine, following researches at Edinburgh into his parents' symptoms. Learning of the new concept of galvanism (creating electrical currents from opposing metals), he surmised that this could have potential medical benefits in cases of palsy, and set about constructing apparatus for his uncle to use. A set of galvanic plates was subsequently dispatched to Balgonie together with instructions on their use.[15] Entertainment and amusement also justified scientific experimentation (as they would later in Perth). His sisters and another female relative in Kincardine received a camera obscura that he constructed, together with focusing instructions. This precursor of photography would enable them, he claimed, to 'exhibit a beautiful & animated representation of the objects before it'.[16]

Anderson's known mathematical and accounting skills were also increasingly solicited for practical, business purposes. Even as a student at St Andrews his education led to involvement in the family's shipping interests. In 1802, on his father's behalf and in his name, he drafted correspondence for a reduction in the price of a timber consignment.[17] Four years later, he provided a detailed calculation of the burthen of a new sloop, and later the same year embarked on a lengthy negotiation over a claim against the family by an English customer for an outstanding debt relating to a disputed cargo destination. Following careful investigation, the claim was determined by Anderson to be justified and the threat of expensive litigation averted with payment and an apology. Relations with his elder brother, John, were strained however, by Anderson's subsequent repeated strictures that memory could be trusted for facts, but was 'a very unsafe guide in money transactions, and figures in general, where regular documents are wanting.'[18]

Mathematical skills could also be tapped for land measurement and surveying. In 1803, a 'Mr Hunter' (possibly of Blackness, Dundee), an acquaintance who had a territorial dispute with a neighbour over a river, sought his help. Anderson drew a plan for Hunter, which was at variance with that produced by his neighbour's surveyor. The Court of Session appointed John Ainslie (1745-1828), Scotland's most eminent surveyor, to check the survey submitted by Hunter. To Anderson's delight, he secured Ainslie's verification, leading him to predict confidently that the Session would give its verdict to Hunter. He derived particular satisfaction from the fact that Ainslie had enquired of his methodology (apparently calculated entirely by the chain) and had reputedly described it as 'one of the best drawn & most accurate plans that he had met with.'[19] Three years later, in July 1806, Anderson became embroiled again in estate management, on this occasion to his personal inconvenience. Prior to leaving Edinburgh for Angus, he had hoped to visit his parents at Kincardine, but his visit was placed in jeopardy, since he had 'a great deal to do in the calculations of Mr Greenhill's Estate' before he left. The task had been undertaken from gratitude and doubtless from a frank recognition of the need to cultivate Greenhill's continuing goodwill. He grumbled that, if he had foreseen its extent, he would not have accepted the commitment, but since it was his own choosing, he could not give it up before the work was finished.[20]

Anderson received regular reminders of financial constraint. Inevitably in Edinburgh books proved a particular temptation, since bargains appeared in auctions. In June 1804, a twenty-volume encyclopaedia - probably the third edition of the *Britannica*, published with supplements between 1788 and 1801 - was available for less than half of the normal retail price; to his frustration, he lacked the means of purchase.[21] A year later, he was embarrassed when former, 'mainly grown-up', fellow students of a higher mathematics class that he had attended, resolved to gift their professor a mathematical instrument costing £120. He was loathe to part with his allocated equal share of 5 guineas, but did not wish to be 'singular', especially since the intended beneficiary was 'a very worthy & a very learned man'.[22] On another occasion, in a conscious attempt to save money on a return journey to Edinburgh from Kincardine, he walked from the Forth ferry to Falkirk, and then set off on foot for Linlithgow, expecting the coach to overtake him at a saving of 4d for every mile walked. His strategy misfired, since a full coach overtook him, obliging Anderson to share a post-chaise with another traveller costing three shillings more than a coach ticket from Falkirk.[23]

Career ambition and financial motives also led him to accept literary commissions, but these too could prove more time-consuming than anticipated, with resulting feelings of recrimination.

The son of his acquaintance, Mr Hunter, having taken a share in one of the major Edinburgh booksellers, persuaded him to undertake 'a paper or two' for some of the reviews of books or magazines.[24] Whether he did so is uncertain, but in June 1805, on the recommendation of some of the Edinburgh professors, he commenced an explicit commission for Henry (later Sir Henry) Steuart (1759-1836). Best known as author of *The Planter's Guide*, his ideas on estate improvement were tested with some success on his property at Allanton, in Craignethan parish in Lanarkshire. Steuart's literary attainments were also in classics, which earned him an LLD, as well as fellowships of the Royal Society of Edinburgh and the Edinburgh Antiquarian Society. Anderson was contracted to finish part of a book that Steuart was planning to publish imminently. The former calculated that it would cost about a month's labour, at a sacrifice of sleep and leisure, since he could not steal time from his pupils. His expectations of remuneration were limited, though he did expect to be offered at least £10; characteristically, he valued 'the acquaintance of such as Mr Stewart a much greater object than the Emolument'. Almost simultaneously however, he realised that the task might require 'more time and pains' than initially supposed.[25] A month later, Anderson complained that he had not a spare minute, since the commission required immediate dispatch. This was fulfilled, as part of what Steuart admitted were Herculean efforts to prevent 'casual errours' [sic]. Payment took longer to settle. Not until April 1806, following 'the decision of a reference', did Anderson wring £20 out of the author, three times what Steuart offered of his own accord. Even that Anderson felt was still inadequate for the amount of work. In that year Steuart published his very substantial, two-volume work, *The works of Sallust; to which are prefixed two essays on the life, literary character, and writings of the historian, with notes historical, biographical, and critical.*[26] There can be no doubt that Anderson's commission related to this erudite, deeply referenced translation. It was Steuart's only known publication in 1806, or for several years. Proficiency in Latin and Greek would have equipped Anderson well to undertake the task; indeed extensive linguistic skills in both classical languages would have been essential for its fulfilment. Of possible relevance for the future however, it seems unlikely that Anderson could have been unaware that Steuart's writings also included advocacy of canalisation between Glasgow and Edinburgh, as a means of more fully exploiting Lanarkshire's coal resources. Many years later Anderson would be directly involved as a consultant on navigational improvements on the Tay, which addressed similar issues relating to the economic potential of canalisation.

Meantime he had learned an important lesson, 'to guide me in future business transactions, and that is, to leave as little as possible to generosity, and to make sure of a regular bargain.'[27] Years later he would never be coy about demanding increased remuneration for teaching and engineering services in Perth. Although he generally stuck by his resolution, judicious exceptions were nonetheless made. In 1807, Principal James Playfair descended on Edinburgh to superintend publication of his six-volume *A System of geography, ancient and modern* (Edinburgh, 1808-1814). He entrusted Anderson with the section on natural history, giving him power to make any corrections and additions he thought appropriate. Under a sense of obligation to the Playfair family for hospitality at St Andrews during his final year as a student there, Anderson devoted time to the task without expectation of pecuniary reward. But, as he shrewdly reflected with an eye to future career prospects, it would make Playfair 'more my friend than ever'.[28]

Anderson's sojourn in Edinburgh coincided with a particularly critical period in the ongoing wars with revolutionary France. Local visits by the press gang highlighted Royal Navy concerns over manpower shortages against the backcloth of the French threat. Even in the comparative tranquility following the Peace of Amiens, a 'hot' press occurred in Leith in spring 1803, in which two hundred men were reputedly snatched and about the same time a member of one press gang died following a fight with the inhabitants.[29] A year later, in circumstances that are unclear, Anderson was actively involved, apparently by his family, in trying to secure the release of an apprentice, David Millar, following the latter's impressment.[30] With the end of the 'armed truce' and renewal of hostilities, fear of a French invasion rapidly escalated to fever pitch. Even in Angus

Anderson discovered, when he accompanied the Greenhills to Old Montrose for the autumn retreat, that watches were now being mounted on the east coast. His maritime knowledge, however, led him to discount the immediacy of invasion, because of the prevalence of strong westerly gales.[31]

Within a few weeks, on his return to Edinburgh, where Lord Moira had arrived to take charge of defence, naval frigates were assembling in the Forth. The previous year Anderson had been in danger of being drafted into the militia at either Kincardine or Balgonie. The prospect was distasteful, and he enthusiastically endorsed his father's proposal for a subscription for insurance against the threat. With thousands, including many of Edinburgh's intellectual elite, rushing to join the Volunteers, he accepted that a contribution to the nation's defence might now be unavoidable. Deploying a pike did not appeal to his scholarly nature as 'a very genteel mode of fighting, but the urgency of the case excuses little delicacies – and we need not stand upon too great ceremony with men who come to rob us, or cut our throats'.[32] Shortly afterwards he was offered a lieutenancy in a corps of pikemen, which he rejected on cost grounds: officers had to provide their own clothing (about £15-20). He was aware nonetheless that those who took no active part would be viewed as disaffected – 'and as this is always a great obstruction to promotion in my profession I fancy I shall yet be under the necessity of taking a pike if not as an officer at least as a private.'[33] Anderson rarely lost focus on future career prospects.

The critical question was, of course, what career to follow. At the outset his tutor post had been viewed as a financial passport to continued theological study and an eventual church vacancy. In April 1804, his second year of divinity at Edinburgh was successfully crowned by passing with another discourse, this time in Latin. That earned 'great applause' from Professor Hunter,[34] which undoubtedly gratified Anderson. The professor, 'an evangelical moderate', enjoyed respect, for a cocktail of conservative Calvinist theology, support for evangelical causes, participation in Edinburgh clubs, and a 'refined liberality'. Hunter's evangelicalism inevitably aroused the wrath of some, however: the quintessential Moderate, Alexander

Carlyle, had not unexpectedly detected that he assisted 'young men of his own fanatical cast'. Anderson was unlikely to have found much common ground with those receiving such favours. More critically, Divinity Hall at Edinburgh University was in poor academic health. Comprising chairs in merely three subjects, only one of which was compulsory, and even lacking, until 1847, a chair in Biblical Criticism, the professoriate of the Faculty was generally considered 'torpid'. The verdict of both Carlyles, from opposite poles of the Calvinist spectrum, was that the student experience was 'dull'.[35] Anderson too clearly found the Faculty uninspiring. His continuing personal religiosity nonetheless remained unambiguous: it suffused his view of the world. Even the credentials of the incoming commander-in-chief for Scotland, Lord Moira, were tested in this light. As a weekly churchgoer, Moira passed, and was pronounced 'a good as well as great man'. Rhetorically, Anderson asked: 'What might be expected from Troops led by a General who conjoins in his character religious experience and fortitude?'[36]

But his religious zeal had no place for bigotry. As a divinity student at St Andrews in 1801, he had heard one of the Haldane brothers from Dundee, pedlars of popular evangelism, and was appalled. The speaker had not only repeated 'their common theme the irregularity & licentiousness of the former part of his life, but spoke very presumptuously as if his calling & election was now sure'. Anderson was distrustful of damascene converts who paraded St Paul as a perfect model for emulation; that approach implied 'the greater Sinner, the greater saint'. Indeed, all religious excess, particularly sectarianism, clashed with his instinctive belief in rational balance and moderation. This extended to differences between the Established Churches of Scotland and England. Thus, although he preferred the discipline of the native Kirk in several respects to that of the Church of England, partly because he felt 'unnecessary observance of forms and dogmas' could distract the mind from the purpose of worship, he recognized that the Anglican communion had 'many worthy members and genuine Christians'. With regard to sects however,

There are two rocks upon which people are
apt to split – when one is blindly devoted
to a particular sect, it narrows the heart and
has a tendency to destroy the noblest
feelings of our nature, and the
characteristic principle of Christianity, I
mean benevolence, and mutual charity. On
the other hand too liberal and extensive
views are in danger of producing
indifference as to form, and indifference as
to the fundamental principles of religion –
The true Christian spirit enables one to sail
between the two and to join the meekness
of charity with the fervour of devotion.

The world would be 'a scene of less strife and more happiness',
when mankind learned the absurdity of persecution, the need for
forbearance, a temperate regard for their own opinions without
casting aspersions on those of others, or inciting jealousies and
religious animosities. God had bestowed differences in intellect, so
slight differences of religious sentiments were 'not incompatible with
appointments of his providence.' Christian forbearance was required,
so that differences became 'lost in eternity'.[38] When curiosity
prompted him to attend the General Session of the Seceders in
Edinburgh, he was struck by their 'utmost rancour and animosity in
controverting the opinions of each other.' They attempted to reason
through quotations from scripture 'totally misinterpreted, twisted
and perverted to serve their own particular views', with an inherent
tendency to slide into division over questions that had no immediate
connection with religious principles. He lamented that 'the Christian
religion which in its nature is so admirably adapted to promote the
peace and comfort of mankind should so often be made the tool of
political intrigue and the source of intoleration [sic] and dissention.'[39]

Personal tolerance and rationalism would have made him a
potentially acceptable candidate for the ministry within the
Established Church during this period of Moderate party

ascendancy. Strongly imbued with the values of the Enlightenment, they too distrusted enthusiasm, championed relative tolerance, and espoused intellectual pursuits. But Anderson's religiosity and sense of social propriety were offended by the worldliness and lifestyles of some clergy, a laxity that was itself already nurturing evangelicalism and religious dissent, and would lead ultimately to an unstoppable demand for regeneration through reconnection with the Kirk's Calvinist roots. Reinforcing disillusionment was the realisation that his prospects of securing a charge were uncertain. By April 1805, his doubts about a clerical vocation had reached crisis point. He confessed to his parents not only that his divinity studies were very little advanced, but also that:

> I never had any particular predilection to be a clergyman, unless as a step to a professorship, which at present I have good reason to think I will soon attain, from a very kind letter I had lately from Principal Playfair . . . I certainly would have no objections to a Kirk and if you are anxious to see me in that line, it is my duty to comply with your wishes . . . I can readily conceive that a good and honest man might still be respected, though a clergyman. But what above all things frightens me, is the idea of hanging on without a settlement – A preacher without friends is certainly a most pitiable object, and a very useless member of society. From their peculiar situation too they are led into tippling, snuffing habits which I detest – you may say, this might be easily avoided, but I know them better, and such practices are inevitable if one wishes to keep on good terms with the clergy – There is but one way of avoiding it, to be presented to a kirk immediately upon quitting college and this falls to the lot of very few.[40]

Negative vibes from the social lifestyle of many Moderate clergy and the insecurity of the 'stickit minister' were complemented, however, by increasing attraction to alternative callings, which in his mind were complementary to religion, not in conflict with it, specifically teaching and science. Again he bared his soul to his parents, describing the conflicting tensions in his mind:

> A scholar runs little pecuniary risks, but his life is far from being free of cares and inquisitions – These however are greatly overbalanced by the pleasures of knowledge, pleasures greatly superior to what the miser enjoys when he has succeeded to the utmost of his wishes in the accumulation of treasure, useless to himself and useless to the world – It is ever to me a source of the purest delight, to trace, & observe the growing progress of my pupils in knowledge and in Virtue – The oldest [Greenhill pupil] will not only do honour to my instructions, but I hope he will be an ornament to human nature – There are times when I think that the pleasures of giving religious instruction, or a conscientious discharge of the off[ice?] of a minister, would yield the truest enjoyment upon earth; at other times I am carried away by a love of a science, and a thirst for knowledge, which are in a great measure precluded by the clerical life – But my ultimate object in either case is to trace the works of God, as they are manifested in the moral or physical world – Even a philosopher with all his knowledge, without the comfortable doctrines of Christianity is little to be envied.[41]

If Anderson's mind had ever been truly directed towards a clerical calling that settled preference no longer existed. His true commitment, he now realized, was to scholarship. He was thankful that he enjoyed 'the means of increasing my knowledge and improving my mind', having come to this through 'some little tribulation & difficulty'. Money was not, he averred, a major anxiety – perhaps he was 'not destined to possess much of it.' The cultivation of his intellectual faculties had now become 'all the happiness we can expect in this world – more, would make us indifferent about the next.'[42]

Although the Church would no longer provide the stepping stone, Anderson's goal of an academic appointment remained intact; and St Andrews still appeared the most accessible avenue. At Edinburgh Anderson continued to maintain contact with former professorial contacts in Fife. During a visit to St Andrews in June 1804, he was warmly received, especially by Principal Playfair of United College, who insisted that he slept at his house. Anderson was fully aware that the latter was challenging the regime of Dr Hill, Principal of the University, and the latter's predilection for filling vacant chairs with relations and associates. He had no personal objection to one or two Hill acolytes gaining chairs, 'but monopolies of professorships are as dangerous to the public as monopolies of corn; the one tends to starve the mind the other the body.' Optimistically, he hoped that Playfair would prevail.[43] Two years later, by which time his clerical ambitions had been firmly jettisoned, his interest in St Andrews acquired a more direct focus. In April 1806, he anticipated a communication from Greenhill on the subject of a professorship at St Andrews, and was convinced that his employer would do all in his power to promote his candidature without any solicitation on his own behalf. This probably related to hopes of a filling the chair in mathematics in place of its ailing holder, but a month later 'Old Vilant' still held out 'as toughly as ever'. By then Anderson had a second string at St Andrews, since Playfair had advised him that there were moves afoot to found a class of chemistry, with funding provided by George Dempster of Dunnichen (1732-1818), the Angus agriculturist, politician and former student of St Andrews, who lacked a near heir. Playfair hinted that Anderson might have a good chance of the first appointment, if such a development took place.[44] A year later, in March 1807, Anderson's hopes were fading: Vilant might 'drop off', but he anticipated that Hill would secure the situation 'for some of his friends'. This prediction proved at least partly true. Within three months Vilant died and Anderson had to accept that all chance of the vacancy had gone. In a diatribe against the nepotism and corruption of the ancien regime, exemplified by the Hills, he complained that 'the present men in power disregard every thing, but themselves and their friends'. Hill and his associates had raised a cry of 'no Popery' to serve their own selfish purposes, but 'Dr Hill would have addressed the Pope as readily had he thought it would increase his own political influence.' Anderson's only consolation was his belief that Hill had been 'half-convicted of double-dealing' by his own party, had lost the confidence of his political patron, Lord Melville, and that, as a result, one of his relations would not succeed Vilant.[45] Yet, however instructive this lesson in the criticality of influence in academic appointments in the early nineteenth century, it did not help Anderson to realize his own ambitions. Three decades would elapse before he could mobilize sufficient political influence on his own behalf to secure a St Andrews chair.

If a university post was attractive, the immediate reality was that Anderson was still a family tutor. His aptitude in that role emerged early. In September 1803, Anderson and his charges were due to return to Edinburgh, when the two older boys would be admitted respectively to Edinburgh University and the High School. Greenhill was uncertain whether the third and youngest, David, who was also Anderson's pupil, should be sent to Edinburgh, but his tutor enthused at the 'astonishing' progress that the latter had made in a few weeks at Montrose.[46] Back in Edinburgh Anderson resisted family importunities to make home visits to Kincardine; his prime responsibility, he insisted conscientiously, was to his pupils. Excusing himself in July 1805, he noted that pupils attending the High School were awarded prizes according to their standing in class, and that his presence was therefore absolutely necessary to keep the middle boy as high as possible till the examination. He acknowledged that Greenhill would estimate the success of his teaching by that standard

– 'and although I am conscious to myself, of giving his sons all manner of justice, yet I acknowledge, besides the approbation of my own mind, I would like also that of my employer.'[47] The following year Anderson's dedication paid dividends when the youngest Greenhill boy, who also attended the High School by then, was head of his class – 'a very pleasing circumstance . . . and I dare say, is no less so to his father.' This, he reflected, was the highest honour that a boy of his age could attain in Scotland. Greenhill was equally impressed with his sons' progress and commissioned Anderson to take them as a reward to Glasgow, taking in Lanark, the Falls of Clyde, and Hamilton Palace, before returning to Edinburgh by a different route. This four-day jaunt used the expensive mode of travelling by chaise, at the substantial cost of twenty guineas. Anderson enjoyed it, noting with satisfaction that he had nothing to pay.[48] Continued vigilance was required nonetheless; a few months later, in August 1806, his young protégé still needed Anderson's 'constant attendance ...to make a respectable figure at the public Examination.'[49]

By then Anderson had been in the Greenhills' employment for four years, a period that had been life changing. His vocation for a clerical calling had proved shallow. Anderson's commitment was clearly to scholarship, but a university appointment seemed as remote as ever. At the same time he was hard-headed financially: 'a poor scholar is not only a helpless member of Society, but often exposed to contempt & pity, two things which a man of a liberal education can worst submit to be the object of.'[50] The young Greenhills would require a family tutor for sometime, so his employment remained secure, but desperation for a change of any kind was increasingly evident. In June 1805, he privately entertained hopes of being offered a tutorial post with the influential Maule family, but felt that attempts to solicit a firm offer would be counter-availing.[51] Four months later he even toyed with an offer to accompany a young gentleman to Germany 'more as a friend and companion than a Tutor'. If accepted, he would reside one year at Dresden in Saxony, before embarking on a grand tour of Europe, a total engagement of three or four years. All expenses would be paid and if allowed a salary of £100 a year, Anderson confessed that he would be strongly tempted to resign his existing situation. His parents were asked for advice by return, as he had only days to decide.[52] Whether the offer was withdrawn or refused is unknown, but Anderson's level of frustration was clear. For a young person in the relatively modest and ambivalent role of family tutor, his abilities had been recognized by a number of influential patrons, who utilized them in literary and practical projects. Anderson's self-confidence, ambition, and innate skills could only have been nurtured by such attention and experience. In turn, they could no longer be satisfied by the comparatively limited demands and rewards of a family tutor post. Equally important, he had also learned how to work the contemporary system of political and social patronage to his advantage. He was now equipped and eager to face new challenges.

NOTES

[1] Univ. St And. Libr., Spec. Coll., MS38329/32. A. Anderson to parents, [Old Montrose], 6 Aug. 1804; Alex. J. Warden: *Angus or Forfarshire, the land and people*, 5 vols. (Dundee: Charles Alexander, 1880-85), vol. 4, 330-1

[2] M. Cosh: *Edinburgh, the golden age*, (Edinburgh: John Donald, 2003), 135-7, 156-9, 229.

[3] Univ. St And. Libr., Spec. Coll., MS38329/16. A. Anderson to parents, Edinburgh, 25 Jan. 1803; MS38329/33. Same to same, Edinburgh, 6 Nov. 1804; MS38329/39. Same to same, Edinburgh, 13 Oct. 1805.

[4] Univ. St And. Libr., Spec. Coll., MS38329/19. Same to same, Edinburgh, 30 Apr. 1803.

[5] Univ. St And. Libr., Spec. Coll., MS38329/35. Same to same, Edinburgh, 21 May 1805.

[6] Univ. St And. Libr., Spec. Coll., MS38329/13. Same to Andrew Anderson, sen., Balgonie, 8 Sep. 1802; MS38329/14. Same to same, Edinburgh, 13 Nov. 1802; MS38329/17. Same to parents, Edinburgh, 11 Mar. 1803.

[7] Univ. St And. Libr., Spec. Coll., MS38329/16. Same to same, Edinburgh, 25 Jan. 1803.

8   Univ. St And. Libr., Spec. Coll., MS38329/18. Same to Andrew
    Anderson, sen., Edinburgh, 18 Apr. 1803; MS38329/21. Same to
    uncle [John Moon], Old Montrose, 11 Sep. 1803;NAS.,
    CH2/40/12, Minutes of the Presbytery of Brechin, 11 Nov. 1802,
    6 Apr. 1803.

9   Univ. St And. Libr., Spec. Coll., MS38329/18. A. Anderson to
    Andrew Anderson, sen., Edinburgh, 18 Apr. 1803; MS38329/37.
    Same to parents, Edinburgh, 14 July 1805; R. N. Smart,
    Biographical register of the University of St Andrews 1747-1897,
    (St Andrews: [University of St Andrews Library], 2004), 662.
    The well-endowed academy at Inverness originated in 1787-92,
    offering a scientific curriculum based closely on the Perth
    Academy model. (K. Macdonald, *The History of the Inverness
    Royal Academy*, (Inverness: Printed by R. Carruthers & Sons,
    1906), 5-7.

10 Univ. St And. Libr., Spec. Coll., MS38329/22. A. Anderson to
    parents, Old Montrose, 11 Oct. 1803.

11 Xerox copy of printed list of *Subscribers of Edinburgh Subscription
    Library, 22 November 1808*, in author's possession. Information on
    date of admission, 3 December 1800, kindly extracted from the
    library's minute books by Dr L. Williams, University of Dundee.

12 A. Grant, *The Story of Edinburgh University, during its first three
    hundred years*, (London: Longmans, Green & Co., 1884), vol. 1,
    320.

13 Univ. St And. Libr., Spec. Coll., MS38329/22. A. Anderson to
    parents, Old Montrose, 11 Oct 1803; MS38329/19. Same to same,
    Edinburgh, 30 Apr. 1803.

14 Univ. St And. Libr., Spec. Coll., MS38329/22. Same to same, Old
    Montrose, 11 Oct. 1803.

15 Univ. St And. Libr., Spec. Coll., MS38329/19. Same to same,
    Edinburgh, 30 Apr. 1803; MS32389/21. Same to uncle [John
    Moon], Old Montrose, 11 Sep. 1803.

16 Univ. St And. Libr., Spec. Coll., MS38329/31. Same to parents,
    Edinburgh, 27 July 1804.

17 Univ. St And. Libr., Spec. Coll., MS38329/8. Andrew Anderson,
    sen. to Mr Stephenson, Kincardine, 14 June 1802.

18 Univ. St And. Libr., Spec. Coll., MS38329/42. A. Anderson to parents, Edinburgh, 9 July 1806; MS38329/48. Same to Andrew Anderson, sen., Edinburgh, 30 Apr. 1807 [and other correspondence in MS38329].

19 Univ. St And. Libr., Spec. Coll., MS38329/22. Same to parents, Old Montrose, 11 Oct. 1803. This dispute has not proved traceable in the official records of the Court of Session.

20 Univ. St And. Libr., Spec. Coll., MS38329/42. Same to same, Edinburgh, 9 July 1806.

21 Univ. St And. Libr., Spec. Coll., MS38329/29. Same to same, Edinburgh, 16 June 1804.

22 Univ. St And. Libr., Spec. Coll., MS38329/37. Same to same, Edinburgh, 14 July 1805.

23 Univ. St And. Libr., Spec. Coll., MS38329/44. Same to same, Edinburgh, 7 Nov. 1806.

24 Univ. St And. Libr., Spec. Coll., MS38329/25. Same to same, Edinburgh, 25 [Jan?] 1804.

25 Univ. St And. Libr., Spec. Coll., MS38329/36. Same to same, Edinburgh, 16 June 1805.

26 Sallust, *The works of Sallust; to which are prefixed two essays on the life, literary character, and writings of the historian, with notes historical, biographical, and critical*, by Henry Steuart (London: Printed for C. and R. Baldwin by James Ballantyne, Edinburgh, 1806). The author's foreword was dated December 20, 1805. In the book's preface, Steuart commented on the 'considerable pains' that had been bestowed on proof correction, and noted that 'the labour of minute, and accurate reference, particularly to the ancient authors, is known only to those, who have themselves attempted the practice'. (vol. 1, x-xi)

27 Univ. St And. Libr., Spec. Coll., MS38329/37. A. Anderson to parents, Edinburgh, 14 July 1805; MS38329/40. Same to same, Edinburgh, 10 Apr. 1806. For background on Steuart, see http://www.bonkle.org.uk/bonkle/allanton.htm.

28 Univ. St And. Libr., Spec. Coll., MS38329/51. A. Anderson to parents, Edinburgh, 31 July 1807.

29   Univ. St And. Libr., Spec. Coll., MS38329/17. Same to same, Edinburgh, 11 Mar. 1803; MS38329/18. Same to Andrew Anderson, sen., Edinburgh, 18 Apr. 1803.

30   Univ. St And. Libr., Spec. Coll., MS38329/25. Same to parents, Edinburgh, 25 Jan. 1804.

31   Univ. St And. Libr., Spec. Coll., MS38329/22. Same to same, Old Montrose, 11 Oct. 1803.

32   Univ. St And. Libr., Spec. Coll., MS38329/11. Same to Andrew Anderson, sen., Balgonie, 28 Aug. 1802; MS38329/23. Same to John Anderson, Edinburgh, 5 Nov. 1803.

33   Univ. St And. Libr., Spec. Coll., MS38329/24. Same to parents, 25 Dec. 1803.

34   Univ. St And. Libr., Spec. Coll., MS38329/26. Same to same, Edinburgh, 12 Apr. 1804.

35   A. Grant, *op.cit.*, vol. 1, 335-37; Ian Campbell, 'Carlyle and the University of Edinburgh' in *Four centuries: Edinburgh University life, 1583-1983*; ed. by Gordon Donaldson (Edinburgh: University of Edinburgh, 1983), 62; *Oxford Dictionary of National Biography* (Oxford: OUP, 2004), vol. 28, 889 (article on Andrew Hunter, by D. F. Wright); *Dictionary of Scottish church history & theology*; ed. by Nigel M. de S. Cameron (Edinburgh: T & T Clark, 1993), 417 (article on Hunter).

36   Univ. St And. Libr., Spec. Coll., MS38329/27. A. Anderson to parents, Edinburgh, 25 Apr. 1804.

37   Univ. St And. Libr., Spec. Coll., MS38329/4. Same to same, St Andrews, 18 Apr. 1801.

38   Univ. St And. Libr., Spec. Coll., MS38329/37. Same to same, Edinburgh, 14 July 1805.

39   Univ. St And. Libr., Spec. Coll., MS38329/41. Same to same, Edinburgh, 17 May 1806.

40   Univ. St And. Libr., Spec. Coll., MS38329/34. Same to same, Edinburgh, 21 Apr. 1805.

41   Univ. St And. Libr., Spec. Coll., MS38329/36. Same to same, Edinburgh, 16 June 1805.

42   Univ. St And. Libr., Spec. Coll., MS38329/38. Same to same, Edinburgh, 25 July 1805.

43   Univ. St And. Libr., Spec. Coll., MS38329/28. Same to same, Edinburgh, 6 June 1804.

44   Univ. St And. Libr., Spec. Coll., MS38329/40. Same to same, Edinburgh, 10 Apr. 1806; MS38329/41. Same to same, Edinburgh, 17 May 1806.

45   Univ. St And. Libr., Spec. Coll., MS38329/46. Same to same, Edinburgh, 26 Mar. 1807; MS38329/50. Same to same, Edinburgh, 9 June 1807.

46   Univ. St And. Libr., Spec. Coll., MS38329/21. Same to uncle [John Moon], Old Montrose, 11 Sep. 1803.

47   Univ. St And. Libr., Spec. Coll., MS38329/38. Same to parents, Edinburgh, 25 July 1805.

48   Univ. St And. Libr., Spec. Coll., MS38329/40. Same to same, Edinburgh, 10 Apr. 1806; MS38329/41. Same to same, Edinburgh, 17 May 1806.

49   Univ. St And. Libr., Spec. Coll., MS38329/43. Same to same, Old Montrose, 16 Aug. 1806.

50   Univ. St And. Libr., Spec. Coll., MS38329/42. Same to same, Edinburgh, 9 July 1806.

51   Univ. St And. Libr., Spec. Coll., MS38329/36. Same to same, Edinburgh, 16 June 1805.

52   Univ. St And. Libr., Spec. Coll., MS38329/39. Same to same, Edinburgh, 13 Oct. 1805.

3

THE 'BUSINESS OF EDUCATION' IN MIDDLE-CLASS PERTH

By 1807 Anderson was determined to move on, and in May, if not earlier, was actively manoeuvring to be appointed an assistant to Alexander Gibson, rector of Perth Academy since 1779: the post, he hoped, would be secured without much difficulty. Although Gibson already had one assistant, he was reputedly 'not considered sufficiently respectable to succeed to the Rectorship.' Anderson's real ambition in pursuing the assistantship was to secure the longer-term succession to the more senior post. His candidature was promoted with vigour, as he sought to gain and deploy influence through personal contacts and a charm offensive. A 'Mr Honey' – almost certainly John Honey from Scone, a contemporary from his days at United College and St Mary's - introduced him to 'several genteel people' in the vicinity of the city, who invited him to their houses. In addition, Anderson made a point of attending a public ball, frequented by 'the first people in the town'. Somewhat immodestly he confided to his parents that he was complimented on his appearance and, in other respects too, the canvass had not been devoid of pleasure. He had elicited support from David Moncrieff, minister of Redgorton, a man of considerable landed property, independent of his stipend. Of particular interest, the latter had two 'beautiful and amiable' daughters, effectively heiresses to his fortune. In addition, Anderson had enjoyed a social outing with Honey and two other local belles, the Misses Lawson, taking careful note that each had a tocher of £10,000. Apart from being 'well-looked', all four ladies had received a 'good & religious education'; only partly perhaps in humour, he speculated on future attachments and triumphantly confided in his parents, that 'from all this you may see I have more inducements than one for wishing a settlement at Perth.'

Concurrently urging discretion over his prospects at Perth Academy, Anderson counselled his parents that secrecy in business was 'the next thing to experience & address'.[1] In the early nineteenth century, however, these recommendations were rarely sufficient. Influence was the key that unlocked doors and, as always, Greenhill influence could be enlisted. Charles Greenhill's brother-in-law, the sheriff of Forfar, had relations on Perth Town Council, who, he was sure, would support Anderson's candidature. In June the Anderson lobby was 'trying to bring matters to a bearing',[2] but at the end of the following month, despite a further visit to the city, matters were still unresolved. Gibson negotiated hard to secure his assistant for the smallest salary possible, leading Anderson to complain that the rector was 'extremely fond of money, and little disposed to part with a farthing he can possibly save.' In this stalemate, the rector of the separate Grammar School, William Dick, with whom he had first had contact over the post, made Anderson an offer of a salary of £90 a year to become his own assistant and thus fill a vacancy that had arisen the previous year. Five years before, whilst still a student at St Andrews, Anderson had demonstrated possible interest in a vacant assistantship at the Grammar School,[3] but by 1807 his eyes were set firmly on the science-based Academy, not on the classical seminary. Following further negotiations however, the city's lord provost eventually could confirm the council's offer of the assistant post at the Academy, indicating that the council would allow £25-30 more for a class on chemistry and that the fees might provide a further £30. The total remuneration in this counter-offer still left Anderson in two minds whether to accept:

> I would have to defray the expense of Apparatus and substances for the experiments which would be 10 pounds – On the whole however it might gross 120 or 130 pounds yearly – I have not yet given any final reply, but I don't think I will accept of it – Dick says he has no doubt of its leading to the Rectorship of the

Academy but this though probable is not certain. I think I shall yet get Gibson to agree to some kind of settlement. I might almost engage to allow him within 50 pounds of his average present income, and take my chance – For I am persuaded by diligence & attention I could bring more students to attend the Academy, and with teaching Chemistry could make out a tolerable livelihood in the mean time, and with the certainty of the Succession at his death might live comfortably enough.[4]

Anderson's negotiating skills and determination eventually paid off, but not for two years. Matters finally came to a head in 1809, when the aging Gibson, by now in his mid-sixties, formally requested the council for 'some relief from the fatigue of teaching every hour', by appointing a second assistant and thereafter selecting a successor between the existing one and a new appointee. Further negotiations induced Gibson to resign the rectorship on 8 July, on condition that he would retain £50 of his salary annually as long as he lived.[5] A month later, on 7 August, the local council confirmed Anderson's appointment.[6] Still based in Edinburgh, he translated directly from his family tutorship to headship of one of Scotland's most prestigious schools while still in his twenties. In the early nineteenth century, as the parallel example of the thirty-three year old Thomas Arnold at Rugby demonstrated, such accelerated promotion without extensive classroom teaching or administrative experience was not unknown. In moving from Edinburgh to Perth Anderson emulated the example of many, mainly private adventure, teachers, who migrated north about this time. Perth's Georgian 'new town', separation of social levels, and excellent educational provision for the middle classes, all modelled partly on the capital, projected a comfortingly familiar image.[7] To Anderson, moreover, the city was no stranger, since he had sometimes accompanied his uncle from Balgonie on his visits to town.

When Anderson arrived in Perth in 1809, the academy was nearly fifty years old. Founded by the local council in 1761 under pressure from an enthusiast for natural science, the Reverend John Bonar, Established Kirk minister of the West Church, it was also inspired strangely by English dissenting academies which appealed to the burgh's substantial minority of seceders from the Church of Scotland. Exploiting Perth's locational advantages the school was intended as a break with the past, an economical and less time-consuming alternative to the traditional university, a college providing a highly-concentrated scientific and commercial syllabus, more in tune with the practical needs of the middle classes of an expanding linen centre. As the university system of the eighteenth century eventually responded to changing contemporary needs, Bonar's original ideal became diluted when academies proliferated elsewhere; but while dropping part of its initial theoretical content, Perth Academy at least remained largely faithful to his concept. The long-established grammar school had not been incorporated, nor did the academy compete in teaching classical subjects. The city's determination to acquire an institution of university status was not new, an attempted transplant of St Andrews University to Perth in the 1690s having failed. Yet, despite criticism of traditional universities implicit in Bonar's proposals, subjects taught in them and in the academy overlapped considerably.[8] It was not surprising that Anderson's penultimate predecessor, Dr Robert Hamilton, departed to become professor of natural philosophy at Aberdeen's Marischal College in 1779 or that Anderson and several other academy teachers followed in due course to university chairs. Likewise, it was readily explicable that Anderson, frustrated in his attempt to secure a university chair, should regard Perth Academy with its demanding academic standards of scholarship as the least unacceptable alternative.

By contrast with his own predecessor, Alexander Gibson had appeared less outstanding, despite a local reputation in mathematics and physics.[9] Nevertheless, his thirty-year tenure culminated in the academy's transfer from cramped accommodation above the corn mercat to purpose-built rooms in the 'new town'. Designed by Robert Reid and occupied two years before Anderson's arrival, the new school building comprised the central showpiece of Rose Terrace, fronting the spacious North Inch and bringing under one roof the scatter of seminaries patronised by the council. Included were English, French, writing, drawing and painting, as well as the grammar school. Less happily the new building had appalling acoustics – a source of complaint from Gibson, and perhaps a further spur to his retirement – as well as inadequate heating and cellars prone to inundation when the Tay was in spate. The various schools also remained organically separate, with staff relations characterised by jealousy, pupil poaching, and disputes over teaching hours and accommodation.[10] In this regime the new rector would be *primus inter pares*.

Prior to appointment Anderson had confidently predicted, as noted above, that he would bring more students to the academy. Two years later however, he was forced to admit that the number of boys at the school was not as great as he had expected, though they were five times more numerous than Gibson had attracted in his first year of teaching. Students were still coming, so he anticipated that he would reach 'little short of the average number' in 1809. The real challenge facing Anderson was attributable paradoxically to emulation of the innovative Perth Academy model elsewhere:

> The number of establishments of the same kind throughout the country is now so great that it will require good management, and superior methods of teaching to attract strangers from a distance – Of all kinds of labour literary labour is the worst paid, and I am sure, were I to bestow half the thought on the business of any other profession, I would make more than double the income – It is respectable to be sure and that is some compensation, but respectability alone will make but a hungry kitchen.[11]

Anderson was determined that 'one way and another', he would 'make out pretty well'. Diligence and a business-like approach were clearly required, but the new broom's first initiative backfired. In 1810, unabashed at the prospect of ruffling influential feathers, he unsuccessfully demanded that Perth Subscription Library return books that he claimed erroneously were academy property.[12] More profitably, he persuaded his council employers to join private subscribers in purchasing a staggering £240 worth of equipment for the school, partly by advancing money himself. This gambit was to be deployed again, but it embodied risks: in 1839, two years after he had moved on to St Andrews, the council felt bound to relieve him of advances made on behalf of defaulting subscribers who could no longer be legally pursued. By 1812 nonetheless, presses to house chemistry apparatus were installed and chemical agents bought. Concurrently, plans were afoot to give chemistry, tentatively introduced in 1806 under Gibson as the leading edge science of the time, a permanent place in the academy's curriculum. The new subject was popularised through public lectures and sandwich courses, assisted by the introduction of a modified version of the Bell monitorial system,[13] but traditional interests were not overlooked. Anderson stressed this point in 1819 in a bid for the mathematics chair at St Andrews, contending that the geometry syllabus at Perth Academy presented 'a more extensive view of the Science than is usually given at our Universities'. Simultaneous success by former pupils in uplifting mathematics prizes at St Andrews and Edinburgh lent some credence to the claim.[14]

Vocational skills in teaching were the key. Presentations from grateful pupils, the first of a silver cup only a year after his appointment, reflected their reaction to a style of teaching that 'had rather attracted than impelled them to their literary labours'. A subsequent gift of a working model of a steam engine comprised a particularly convincing double testimony to its effectiveness. Official visitations also documented an increasing roll, the rector's scientific reputation, his communicative abilities and, belatedly, even pupil emulation of his neat handwriting. More important, Anderson's moral ascendancy and control were observed, despite a rejection of contemporary mores of discipline:

There was no reproach, no severity. If a pupil appeared to be inattentive, trifling away his time, and, above all, if any symptoms of vice were observed, his method was to send for him, and in private represent to him the great value of knowledge in guiding a man through the difficulties and intricacies of life — the awful danger of indulging in vicious habits to both body and soul — and then appeal to the manly and nobler parts of his nature — and, after doing all this, in the gentlest and kindest manner dismiss him by stating his firm conviction that from henceforth he was sure that he would never again require to speak to him in this manner. He thus not only effectually corrected what was wrong, but secured ever after the affection and gratitude of the scholar, who would not again willingly give offence to so humane a teacher. Such was the aim and end of the whole man to overcome evil with good.[15]

Teaching skills were complemented by a profound personal commitment to his charges, exemplified in numerous requests to his old friend, Thomas Chalmers, to assist in finding tutorial work for them on arrival at university. Personal experience had taught him that this could ease the financial burden of university attendance.[16]

Relations with the teaching staff were equally sound. A future occupant of a London University chair, William Ritchie, recalled that Anderson's conduct was 'such as scarcely to make him feel that he was only his assistant'.[17] Such tact was a prerequisite to harmony in the seminaries. Anderson reputedly had no personal enemies and, in the view of a lifelong friend, was 'gentle almost to facility'.[18] Yet he was clearly no sycophant, as numerous incidents would later emphasise. His council employers were sufficiently impressed with their new rector, that in 1811 they awarded him an annuity of £50 during his predecessor's lifetime. This was intended to compensate him for the loss of the rector's salary, which had been retained to provide in effect a pension to his predecessor. On Gibson's death in 1814, this supplement was consolidated, since Anderson then became entitled to the full emoluments of the rectorship as guaranteed by the terms of his appointment. Despite the council's gesture, Anderson's satisfaction did not last. A lengthy memorial was subsequently submitted to the council, which though couched in his normal polite, courtly language, argued forcibly that 'more limited provision' was made for the rector's remuneration in Perth than in any comparable institution elsewhere in Scotland. Populated with examples drawn from other seminaries, it proved persuasive and his salary was doubled.[19] Subsequent attempts by the cheese-paring council to offset their generosity by depriving him of his assistant were thereafter frustrated, while he remained insistent that he personally chose his staff, and after a rigorous examination on their attainments.[20] When necessary he publicly pandered to the vanity of the self-elective clique on the council, attributing the schools' success to their 'fostering care and attention'. Yet he could also take them to task for failing to provide prizes for his students and for employing 'certain expressions' in the council chamber, which 'might prove injurious to the schools and the teachers'.[21]

Anderson's reputation was concurrently enhanced by his continuing scientific investigation and scholarship. The Royal Society's *Catalogue of Scientific Papers, 1800-63* lists ten original contributions published between 1812 and 1846, seven of them during his sojourn at Perth Academy. The *Edinburgh Philosophical Journal* was the most frequent recipient, but *Nicholson's Journal* and *Thomson's Annals of Philosophy* also featured, while two items were translated for re-publication in German periodicals. Prime themes included the hygrometric state of the atmosphere, the dew point, barometric measurement of mountain heights, and the illuminating power of coal gas.[22] The same interests dominated other literary productions. In the words of its sub-title, he was one of 'the gentlemen eminent in science and literature', who contributed to David Brewster's *Edinburgh Encyclopaedia*, which appeared in several

British and American editions from 1808. His submissions comprised the sections on the barometer, cold, dyeing, fermentation, evaporation, hygrometry, meteorology, navigation and physical geography. Subsequently he also contributed the article on gas lighting to the seventh edition of *Encyclopaedia Britannica* edited by Macvey Napier in 1842.[23] Despite the absence of any single seminal publication, Anderson's recognition in the wider academic world was evinced in the awards of a fellowship of the Royal Society of Edinburgh in 1820 and of an honorary LL.D. from St Andrews University seven years later. The latter, awarded unanimously, was instigated by Chalmers who occupied a chair there at the time.[24]

The Literary and Antiquarian Society of Perth furnished a platform for the first adumbration of many of Anderson's ideas. Holding office for years, as superintendent of natural history, his breadth of interests was matched only by that of the society. In spite of its name, and typical of such an association, its orbit also embraced scientific pursuits. He became virtually resident lecturer, frequently presenting two papers in the course of an evening on topics as diverse as philology and evaporation from the Tay.[25] Outwith the society too he lectured at public request, while inventions, such as his portable atmometer, further whetted the widespread appetite for popular science. An unusually lucid presentation had wide public appeal, prompting the local press to acclaim his aversion to 'mysticisms' and 'the technical language in which a scientific course of lectures is so generally and inappropriately clothed to a popular audience.'[26] At the academy such high calibre teaching, added to courses of university level, ensured that pupils came from a wide catchment area, as far afield as Calcutta and Nova Scotia. Lord Provost Ross purred approvingly in 1812 over the satisfactory state of 'the business of education' in Perth. Yet, there was a paradox: despite Anderson's efforts to promote its facilities locally, 'relatively few of the younger branches of families in Perth itself were placed under such able tuition'. His very success at reviving Bonar's concept of high academic standards curtailed its value to the generality of the local middle classes. Even the *Perth Courier* coyly admitted that Anderson was criticised for being 'too profound'.[27] The annual prospectus of subjects was certainly aimed at the academically gifted.

This preoccupation was noted too by a later obituarist who conceded that 'his great mind was so familiar with the depths of the subject ... in his elucidations of the elementary parts, he was sometimes apt to go beyond the capacities of his pupils.' The failing was human, but it led to the conclusion that 'as a teacher of youth, he was better fitted for the higher than for the elementary department of science.'[28]

NOTES

[1]   Univ. St And. Libr., Spec. Coll., MS38329/40. A. Anderson to parents, Edinburgh, 24 May, 1807.

[2]   Univ. St And. Libr., Spec. Coll., MS38329/50. Same to same, Edinburgh, 9 June, 1807.

[3]   Univ. St And. Libr., Spec. Coll., MS38329/4. Same to same, St Andrews, 18 Apr. 1801; MS38329/11. Same to Andrew Anderson, sen., Balgonie, 28 Aug. 1802; E. Smart, *History of Perth Academy*, (Perth: Milne, Tannahill & Methven, 1932), 72.

[4]   Univ. St And. Libr., Spec. Coll., MS38329/51. A. Anderson to parents, Edinburgh, 31 July, 1807.

[5]   E. Smart, *op.cit.*, 108-110.

[6]   [Perth: Perth & Kinross Archives at A K Bell Library]. P[erth] T[own] C[ouncil | Min | utes], 7 Aug. 1809.

[7]   A.W. Harding, 'Education in Perthshire to 1872', unpublished Ph.D. thesis, University of Dundee, 1974, vol. 2, 512 note.

[8]   *ibid.*, vol. 1, 238-41. See too D. J. Withrington, 'Education and society in the eighteenth century' in *Scotland in the age of improvement: essays in Scottish history;* ed. by N.T. Phillipson and R. Mitchison, (Edinburgh: Edinburgh U.P., 1970), 177-95.

[9]   PTC Min., 5 July 1779. See too E. Smart, *op.cit.*, 85-6, 116; T.H. Marshall, *History of Perth*, (Perth: John Fisher, 1849), 420.

[10]   E. Smart, *op. cit.*, 80, 94; A.W. Harding, *op. cit.*, vol. 2, 500.

[11]   Univ. St And. Libr., Spec. Coll., MS38329/52. A. Anderson to parents, Perth, 7 Nov. 1809.

12 [Perth: Perth & Kinross Archives at A K Bell Library]. Perth records, Perth Library minute book, vol. 1, 25 Dec. 1810; *Perth Courier*, 20 Dec. 1810.

13 *ibid.*, 20 Sep. 1810, 16 Jan. 1812, 20 Apr., 16 Nov. 1815, 7 Nov. 1839; PTC Min., 3 Nov. 1806, 6 Nov. 1810, 7 Jan. 1811, 6 Jan. 1812, 4 Nov., 2 Dec. 1839.

14 E. Smart, *op.cit.*, 100-1; [Edinburgh:] N[ational] A[rchives of] S[cotland], Melville Castle papers, GD 51/6/2059/2. A. Anderson to Sir P. Murray, Perth, 27 Dec. 1819.

15 A.W. Harding, *op.cit.*,vol.2,501;E. Smart: *op. cit.*,110-11; *Perth Courier*, 21 Dec. 1820, 27 July 1826, 16 July 1835; *Perthshire Advertiser*, 10 Dec. 1846 (obituary).

16 NCL, TCP, CHA 4.7.1. A. Anderson to T. Chalmers, Perth, 24 Oct. 1818.

17 PTC Min., 18 Aug. 1821.

18 [Edinburgh:] N[ational] L[ibrary of] S[cotland], Lee papers, Ms 3441/f375. J. Esdaile to Principal Lee, Perth, 5 June 1837.

19 E . Smart: *op. cit.*, 112-16; PTC Min., 4 Mar. 1811, 6 May, 2 Sep. 1816, 3 Sep. 1821; *Perth Courier*, 13 Sep. 1821.

20 PTC Min., 5 Aug. 1811, 18 Aug. 1821, 24 Oct. 1826, 5 Mar. 1827.

21 *ibid.*, 2 Aug., 3 Oct. 1823, 2 Feb. 1824, 3 June 1833, 17 June 1835; *Perth Courier*, 13 June 1833; [Perth: Perth & Kinross Archives at A K Bell Library.] P[erth]T[own] C[ouncil] Corr[espondence], PE/24. A. Anderson to Lord Provost L. Robertson, Perth, 18 July 1817.

22 Royal Society, *Catalogue of scientific papers (1800-1863)*, (London: Royal Society, 1867), vol. 1, 62-3.

23 *Gentleman's magazine*, 27, (1847), 221; *Dictionary of national biography*, (London: Oxford U.P., 1917), vol. 1, 371; *Perth Courier*, 22 Nov. 1822.

24 Information supplied from the records of the Royal Society of Edinburgh and the University Archives, St Andrews, by Mr W.H. Rutherford and Mr R.N. Smart respectively. See too *Perth Courier*, 4 Oct. 1827; NCL, TCP, CHA 4.65.33. A. Anderson to T. Chalmers, Perth, 3 Nov. 1827.

25   *Perth Courier*, 9 Oct. 1817, 8 Oct. 1818, 25 Jan., 8 and 22 Nov. 1821, 24 Oct. 1826, 29 Nov. 1827, 5 Jan., 8 Nov. 1832; *History of the Literary and Antiquarian Society of Perth, 1784-1881*, (Perth: Literary and Antiquarian Society, 1881), 30-1.

26   *Perth Courier*, 11 June, 22 Oct. 1818, 7 Oct. 1819.

27   *ibid.*, 25 July 1811, 20 Aug. 1812, 20 July 1813, 28 July 1814, 26 July 1821, 25 Oct. 1822, 25 July 1833; *Guide to the city and county of Perth*, 4th ed., (Perth: D. Morison, 1824), 23.

28   *Perthshire Advertiser*, 10 Dec. 1846.

4

A SCIENTIFIC POLYMATH: GAS, WATER AND TAY NAVIGATION

Throughout his first ten years in Perth, Anderson's scientific activities were confined to the octagonal room of the academy, popular lectures and the columns of learned journals. In 1819 however, the local council involved him for the first time in the town's long search for an effective supply of clean water: the pattern for the future was set. Two years later he was dispatched to the Balmanno estate, near Bridge of Earn, to assess the operations of Robert Muttrie, who was seeking financial backing in his quest for coal. That commodity was of almost equal importance to a city dependent primarily on water-borne supplies by a river subject to recurrent freezing in winter. Presumably Muttrie's explorations seemed initially promising, since a municipal subvention was forthcoming, but coal on Perth's doorstep was to prove even more elusive than water.[1] The following year Anderson launched out on a more successful undertaking, the creation of a gas lighting system. This demonstration of a capacity to translate scientific concept into practical application stimulated a clamour for his services on an ever-widening range of issues. In the process he donned the mantle of the city's resident scientific consultant for nearly one-quarter of a century, drawing heavily on knowledge and skills first honed as a student and tutor.

Until 1779, 110 clumsy cruise lamps had provided Perth's street lighting, burning Greenland whale oil and emitting minimal illumination. With shop windows adding little to relieve the gloom, the streets were not surprisingly crime-ridden.[2] From the 1780s, however, crystal globes gradually supplanted the former square lamps that were both dilapidated and expensive to maintain.

Relations between the town and a succession of external contractors from Glasgow, Dundee and Edinburgh were tempestuous, but a slow increase in lamp provision did occur, though this was attributable mainly to the physical expansion of the burgh. The cost to the municipal exchequer also showed a worrying increase, almost four-fold between the 1780s and 1811, when the council gratefully dropped responsibility for lighting into the lap of a newly created police commission.[3] Stimulated by the adoption of gas in other towns, a clamour emerged in 1822 for Perth to follow suit, preferably combined with the even more essential provision of clean water. Though possessing legal powers, meagre financial resources denied the commissioners scope for costly innovation, so in tune with the time, private enterprise was left to fill the breech. As early as 1813 a local company had tentatively publicised the advantages of coal gas, but with the establishment of a new joint-stock concern, the Perth Gas Light Company, in December 1822, the proposition attracted more serious attention. Almost all the projected capital requirement of £10,000 in £25 shares was subscribed within days and the company embarked on its declared objective of installing and serving 186 street lamps and 1500 private supply points. Whilst the concern was strictly private, the board inevitably included many who pulled the levers of political influence. These included Lord Provost Patrick Gilbert Stewart and Robert Ross of Oakbank, two individuals who usually occupied the civic chair for alternate biennial terms. Unique among the directors, however, was one whose reason for inclusion was technical expertise: Adam Anderson.[4]

By late January 1823, at the company's request, he had toured existing gas works at Glasgow, Edinburgh and Berwick. Considerable enthusiasm greeted his subsequent highly detailed report. 'Scientific acquirements', in Provost Stewart's summing-up, had 'peculiarly qualified him for the mission upon which he had been sent, and which he had discharged in a manner equally creditable to his talents as a chemist and engineer.' Armed with Anderson's observations and proposals, a petition for a parliamentary bill was approved. Meantime he deflated any embarrassing local opposition by promoting public support for the project. Lectures on the chemical properties of gases, enlivened by experiments, were held in a room at the academy lit by gas subjected to a new mode of purification that he had just discovered. Despite a discriminatory charge of 10/- for ladies, compared with 15/- for gentlemen, relatively few members of the fair sex worked up enthusiasm to attend the course which dragged out until May; nonetheless, his audiences were 'numerous and respectable'. Supplementary proselytising activities included correspondence to the local press and demonstrations of the effectiveness of gas lighting, culminating in an illumination of the royal arms, a star and inscriptions at the academy for the king's annual birthday celebrations.[5]

A sympathetic public opinion having been forged, an application was made in May 1823 to Perth's civic mandarins for the cattle-market at Canal Street as a site for the proposed gas works. Permission was also sought to open up causeways for piping. On receipt of Anderson's letter affirming no danger to the salmon fisheries (a crucial revenue source for the municipal coffers) or to the inhabitants from the use of water from the town's lade for cooling, the council agreed to put the site to public roup and outlined safety regulations for the company's operations. By October 1824, despite delays due to shortages of materials, the curiosity of onlookers, and a gas explosion in a High Street cellar, pipe-laying and the construction of the gas works — likewise designed by Anderson — were sufficiently advanced to commence a service. Starting with the First Relief Kirk, several shops, and the illumination of the main streets, this extended in little more than a year to the theatre, the Salutation Inn, and the Middle Church. In the last case, Perth's general kirk session prudently co-opted Anderson to the installation committee. Even some weavers' shops were fitted up with gas jets at a cost of 10/- per loom, a considerable outlay justifiable only by the expectation of yet longer hours in a trade whose working day, even by contemporary standards, was a byword. Admiring comments emanated from the local press on 'the singularly beautiful appearance' of Smeaton's eighteenth century bridge after twenty batwing gas burners replaced its former oil lamps. A grateful and highly profitable gas company meantime measured its debt to Anderson by presenting him with three hundred guineas worth of silver plate, a substantial honorarium equivalent to more than three times his official annual salary (excluding fees), at the academy.[6]

By the close of the 1830s most public buildings were supplied with gas, including even the county gaol and justiciary hall, after protracted haggling between town and county over respective shares of the installation costs. From 1828, Greyfriars burying ground in the city centre was also lit to frustrate resurrectionism, and in this instance Anderson successfully intervened to pinpoint deficiencies in the council's original 'economy' scheme, which entailed the placing of only four lamps. As he objected, imperfect illumination in this case was worse than none, giving a false sense of security to the authorities and positively assisting the grave robber. His alternative proposals for eight lights, accompanied by a plan for their preferred disposition within the cemetery, reduced the intervening distance between them from 250 to 60 yards.

Shortly afterwards, evening services became possible for the first time in many churches due to gas lighting, and in the home too nocturnal social life was liberated. As early as 1825 Anderson introduced gas into his first St Leonard's Bank house, partly to demonstrate its safety for domestic use. Two years later a supply was opened up to the many middle-class mansions adorning the slopes of Kinnoull Hill, when the pipe at Bridgend village was extended to James Murray's lunatic asylum. The new facility inevitably introduced some potential hazards: for the first time churches required fire insurance and concern was expressed at the reluctance of some weavers to switch off the supply to their shops at night, despite the presence of combustible materials on their premises. The street lighting revolution was also confined initially to the restricted boundaries of the ancient royalty, leaving areas as central as Kinnoull Street without gas fifteen years after its introduction to the town's mediaeval core, but in the city centre the transformation was remarkable. In 1842, the company's initial target had been easily surpassed with no less than 237 street lamps positioned and their greater effectiveness was clear. Even a decade before, contemporaries alluded to the passing of 'the former sombre appearance of our streets and shops.' Equally gratifying, the thoroughfares became less crime-infested, a trend arrested only in 1841 when gas lighting of the streets was temporarily interrupted.[7]

Considerable pride was generated by the brilliance of the city's lighting and its alleged superiority over that of Edinburgh. Many, including the metropolitan police commission, remarked on this and widely attributed the outcome to Anderson's skill as a chemist. Indeed his reputation travelled to other centres. In 1825 approaches appear to have been made to him to superintend the erection of gas works at Arbroath and Montrose, while the principal London gas companies reputedly solicited his attendance before a projected House of Commons committee to state the results of his experiments on the comparative illuminative qualities of coal gas and oil.[8] Actually it is doubtful whether any such parliamentary assignation was kept: the only recorded enquiry into gas lighting at this time had taken place two years earlier. Likewise, there is no evidence that his involvement with the Perth Gas Light Company extended beyond 1825. For his future reputation that was perhaps all to the good: the architect of the gas system would have been powerless to defuse growing dissatisfaction with the cost of the service. From 1825, allegations were freely aired that tariffs were excessive due to the monopolistic situation. Indecent haste in reducing the company's charges three years later at the first whiff of potential opposition lent weight to the complaints. In 1844, after a rival Perth New Gas Light Company emerged and proposals for municipalisation had been rejected, unbridled competition in the classic traditions of nineteenth century capitalism was soon witnessed. The bitter adversaries were both given freedom to rip up city streets to lay their own networks of pipes, while the older company discovered that it had no legal redress for investment on redundant piping after losing the council contract to its undercutting rival. Anderson had no hand in this unedifying spectacle, but his skill in using gas for visual effect could still be deployed. In October 1836, less than a year before his departure to St Andrews, the annual dinner of the Highland and Agricultural Society of Scotland was scheduled to take place in the riding room of the barracks. The local council wanted to impress the twelve hundred guests with a display that would encourage them to return soon, bringing the spin-off for Perth's economy which their sojourn entailed. The upshot was Anderson's final dramatic public spectacle with gas: as well as five chandeliers hanging from the roof, gas jets were suspended in front of the orchestra in the appropriately symbolic representation of a plough surmounted by crown and ciphers.[9]

Gas lighting had barely been installed when Anderson plunged into another modernising, public venture: the introduction of uniform weights and measures. North of the border these had been largely standardised after 1661, when a Scottish parliamentary commission established exemplars, such as the Linlithgow firlot for dry measure, to serve as national norms. Even within Scotland, however, the eradication of confusion and diversity was incomplete. In 1824, Westminster legislation, the Act 5 Geo. IV. c74, stipulated uniformity throughout the British Empire, and the following year Perth Town Council decided to emulate Perth County by procuring a new set of standard weights and measures. Delays over delivery from the London supplier prompted the council, heeding Anderson's advice, to threaten cancellation of its order, but in August 1826 the new weights eventually arrived. They were deposited in the town's record room for safety, while he made a duplicate set for use in the guild court. Change was still gradual: another four months elapsed before the former town weights at the Shore were replaced.

Since Anderson had already drawn up new tables of annuities for council loans in 1824, it was logical to enlist his enumerative skills with the ramifications of the new legislation, especially once opposition was encountered. So two years later, with his mathematics assistant from the academy, he elaborated the full implications of standardisation in a technical report to the sheriff-depute.[10] Attempting the following year to counter residual prejudice, Anderson published tables 'in a popular form' for converting Linlithgow (also Perthshire) bolls into imperial quarters and vice-versa, as an *Appendix to the report on the weights and measures of Perthshire* (Perth: R. Morison, 1827). This uninviting title and its equally tedious, albeit important contents, did little to smooth over ingrained conservatism.[11] In April 1828, while the Perthshire Farming Society, representing an influential, vested interest, urged universal adoption of the new weights to prevent confusion and fraud, Anderson launched a further personal initiative, a marathon series of gratuitous lectures. The popular appeal of discourses on the theoretical basis of such an abstract subject was unsurprisingly limited, so attendances were poor. Anderson was piqued. Feeling that 'from delicacy' he could hardly engage in self-promotion, he solicited assistance from the magistrates, tartly reminding Lord Provost Robert Ross that he had 'bestowed no small labour on the adjustment of the weights and measures of the City.' Having advanced assurances that his remaining lectures would be illustrated with his own apparatus and 'contain many practical views ... with respect to which it is of considerable importance that the public should be rightly informed', civic endorsement followed. Spurred, moreover, by the insinuation that his services were taken for granted, a public dinner was held for him three months later. Before this assembly of local notables, speakers vied with each other in eulogising Anderson in near hagiographical terms. Typically the provost regretted:

> That Perth offered so little scope for his distinguished abilities — abilities calculated to add lustre to a University, and at the head of which they could be more eminent and useful, and better reward their possessor. It was a distinguishing feature in the Doctor's character that he seemed to hold his information more for the public good than his own aggrandizement, and liberally dispensed more with a view to the interests of mankind than with any regard to his own private emolument.

However exaggerated this homage, particularly in the light of subsequent events, it faithfully reflected his public image with contemporaries. Moreover the event revealed the taproot of such energy: an underlying philosophy of social stability preserved by conservative reform, which could even extend to weights and measures. They were, he averred, interwoven with the whole fabric of civil society, and economic and social order depended on their uniformity and accuracy.[12] These values were to spill readily into other non-scientific activities.

Meantime a more demanding challenge beckoned: the unresolved problem of Perth's inadequate water supply. For centuries drinking water had been drawn from either the river Tay directly or the lade, an artificial mediaeval waterway that diverted water from the river Almond to provide power for the city mills and flood the burgh's former defensive ditches. Following an idea mooted in 1752, though not executed until ten years later, a network of pipes had been laid through the principal streets to distribute water from a reservoir constructed by the lade at Drumhars. Perishable timber was used initially, but replaced from the 1780s with lead piping which fed a number of public wells.[13] Concessionary supplies granted ill advisedly to certain private proprietors, mainly in the elite Watergate, were soon withdrawn as an overloaded system struggled to keep pace with demands for additional outlets during the town's eighteenth-century expansion. These difficulties were compounded by problems in ensuring that the contractors fulfilled their maintenance obligations, together with worries over the inadequacy of filtration at the reservoir. Somehow the system creaked into the nineteenth century under the burdens of escalating demand, irregularity of supply and, above all, increasing concern over the toxicity of the water. By then, unlike mediaeval times, it passed through various industrial establishments on the banks of the lade before reaching the town.[14] Consequently, in the 1820s, criticism of 'this refuse of Printfields and Bleachfields, this vile mixture of all the primary colours, Turkey-red, orange, yellow, green, blue, indigo, and violet', had reached a crescendo. The Perth Courier in particular mounted a sustained campaign to undermine a dwindling residue of public confidence in the purity of the drinking water. This task was facilitated by the emotive claim that two hundred soldiers at the Drumhars barracks washed daily – 'with soap' – at the precise point and time at which water was extracted for the city's breakfast tables.[15]

The obvious solution of drawing on a supply outside Perth was, of course, recognised early. Indeed, the initial proposals of 1752, involved piping water from the Tay through the High Street, and in 1781 Anderson's predecessor, Rector Gibson, had been sent on a water survey of the lands of St Magdalen, south of the burgh. Four years later the council investigated the feasibility of a spring water supply, again without result. John Rennie was then consulted in 1808, and a bill even stemmed from his proposal to divert water from Craigie burn, but this proved as abortive as earlier schemes in 1787 and 1804. Yet, despite frustrations, the intensity and continuity of public interest never wavered; in 1814 the working classes of Leonard Street indicated in desperation that they would even be willing to pay for clean water. Unlike their middle-class counterparts in the northern new town, whose opposition to an assessment for this purpose was reinforced by the knowledge that their servants could readily draw pure water direct from the river at the North Inch, distance from the Tay left the weaving community of the Pomarium suburb totally dependent on the unhygienic lade supply.[16]

Anderson's first direct involvement occurred in 1819, when he submitted a detailed chemical analysis to the Perth council on Clathymore spring at Tibbermore. Although his report indicated water of outstanding purity, the cost of piping six miles to Perth and buying out vested interests, added to a fatally deficient supply in summer, led to the scheme's abandonment. Surveys of other springs in Gask, Letham and Craigie by different land surveyors and engineers followed,[17] but increasingly attention focused on the Almond and the Tay as the most favourable prospects. Again Anderson became embroiled, with a request to determine the levels between the falls at Cromwell Park and Linn of Campsie on the one hand and the town on the other. Unhappily distance and problems in the construction of filter beds in their vicinities cancelled out the advantage of their elevated water levels, which would have obviated the use of pumps to raise a head of water.[18] Yet, if a source of pure water and suitable extraction point downstream from these sites could be identified, as the eminent engineer, James Jardine, observed in 1823, no town was 'so favourably situated as Perth for obtaining an ample supply of pure water from the river by steam engine'.

Faced with a Guildry proposal to use the water power of the lade to pump water from the Tay at the North Inch, Anderson and Jardine were consulted on its feasibility. The sluggish flow of the lade, subject to winter frost, summer drought and a backwater from the river in spate, soon ruled it out as a power source, but Anderson's chemical report delivered the coup-de-grace. Experimental pits dug in the Inch and a trial bore in the river bed north of Smeaton's bridge revealed a sub-stratum of clay producing hard water, strongly lime in content and quite unsuitable for most domestic and culinary purposes. Nonetheless, dissatisfaction over apparent municipal inaction, nurtured as always by the local press and aided by the collapse of the existing system for two entire weeks in 1827, stimulated demands for the flotation of a joint-stock company, on the precedent of the successful gas enterprise, to raise the necessary capital. Anderson considered alternate sites at the upper limit of the North Inch and the northern extremity of Moncreiffe Island, two places where the clay bed was intersected. On several counts, including cost, distance, ease of filtration and water purity, the island site was more attractive. This formed the conclusion of two reports by Anderson and Jardine for the council in 1827-28, but it was an ambitious undertaking. From a proposed filter bed at Moncreiffe Island pipes would need to be laid across the channel of a navigable river and, unlike a previous scheme at Glasgow, they required to be sunk sufficiently deep to preclude disturbance by shipping, floods and tides. At the west bank of the Tay the water would pass through a receiving well to filter intruding sand or clay, before continuing into a reservoir initially earmarked for a site in the coal yards adjacent to Greyfriars burial ground.[19]

With a bill framed on the basis of these proposals, Anderson turned proselytiser, energetically defending the capacity of his island filter to deal with the town's rubbish which was regularly dumped in the river upstream from the intended extraction point. To forestall public anxiety over the proximity of the proposed water works to Greyfriars, however, he persuaded the council to bow to public opinion and transfer the site southwards to align with Marshall Place. No engine with ball and socket joints could guarantee accurate jointing indefinitely and he feared that 'malicious or whimsical persons might have it in their power to agitate the public mind, from time to time, with the utmost revolting reports respecting the quality of the water.' Rather than attempt to counter prejudice, it seemed prudent in this instance to defer to it.[20] With a similar combination of firmness and flexibility the council overcame opposition from the northern suburbs to the inevitable assessment on property values, from the salmon fishing interests who feared disruption of their activities during construction, and from the Guildry and trades to the political composition of the projected water commission, which was weighted initially in favour of the ancien regime on the council. This was a formidable task. Conceding the strength of opposition to an assessment, the *Perth Courier* urged the council to make a fiscal contribution to defuse it. The civic rulers, it argued, could hardly contend that public property was so locked up, when thousands could be concurrently spent ornamenting the exterior of a church, St John's, while giving only 'countenance' to a matter the members admitted was 'of vital influence to the comforts and prosperity of the city.'[21]

At its first meeting the new water commission recognised Anderson's contribution, inviting him to attend all subsequent deliberations and advise on the future management and execution of the project. Four months later, with Jardine's unreserved concurrence, he was formally requested to assume overall charge as superintending engineer. Detailed specifications of the diameter, weight and length of all piping, including over five miles of pipes for the city streets, and of a cast iron cistern, destined to hold seven hundred tons of water, were produced. These followed careful surveys to ensure adequate and regular supplies at each proposed public well throughout the year at minimal cost. Drawings of ball and socket joints used on the Clyde were obtained, from which he designed an improved version for the Tay. Laid in forty-five foot lengths, six feet below the river bed, by the unremitting exertions of fifty or sixty men working in relays day and night, the river pipes were equipped with valves to allow a velocity of water from the reservoir to periodically flush out any intruding sediments without recourse to raising them for cleaning. The use of gravity and minimal reliance on pumping were guaranteed by sinking the foundations of the iron receiving wells at the pumping house, twenty-three feet below the floor of the engine-room and fully four feet below the lowest level of the river bed. Due to heavy floods in 1830, about twenty men were required at one point to man pumps constantly, to keep the foundations clear of water. Economy also dictated the inclusion of a mechanical device in the engine-room to raise the effective water level fifteen feet above the nominal maximum level in the cistern, while skilful use of steam from the boiler prevented freezing in cold weather. A mercurial gauge permitted the attendant engineer to know the water level to an accuracy of one-half inch without inspecting the tank.

Anderson also proved to be a passable architect, designing both the engine-house and reservoirs. With the change to a more conspicuous location in line with the Georgian terrace of Marshall Place and the frequently-canvassed, if as yet unbuilt, Tay Street, the relatively utilitarian and economical plans he submitted at the close of 1829 were rejected. These were founded on the premise that 'the appearance of the reservoir would indicate bad taste, as well as an unnecessary waste of the public money, were any attempt to represent it to be greatly different from the real object it is intended to serve.' The final design, adopted in 1830, for an additional outlay of £485, incorporated nine hundred tons of masonry. Built in the Doric style, the unique cast iron dome was ornamented with pilasters, a cornice and frieze adorned with the city arms, and some Ionic features.[22] Although an inspector of works, John Turnbull, was appointed in May 1830, to control day-to-day operations, Anderson retained direct supervision of overall construction. He personally amended plans in response to unforeseen problems, such as planking for the foundations of the chimney stalk, and also vetted all estimates and accounts. The contractors represented a wide geographical spread from Tayside to Cardiff, but the most prominent role fell to Dundee Foundry which supplied piping, one of two steam engines and the cistern. By October 1830, the foundation problems were over, the reservoir taking shape, the filter bed nearly finished and excavation of the river bed to accommodate the great pipe proceeding rapidly. The following May, on behalf of fellow proprietors at St Leonard's Bank, Anderson persuaded the commission to set the precedent of allowing water supplies to private houses: an avalanche of requests followed. Within sixteen months several industrial and commercial concerns in Perth also obtained large quantities of water daily. These included 400 gallons for the Salutation Inn, 670 gallons for the still comparatively small Pullar's dye house, and 2,000 gallons for Provost John Wright's brewery, easily the largest single consumer. Although Anderson was to continue supervising the water works until January 1837, the system as originally conceived was completed by the close of 1834 at a cost of £13,609-11-11½d, and defrayed by a legal assessment or rate on the real rent of occupied houses.[23]

One problem remained, but it proved for the water commissioners unexpectedly thorny: an appropriate fee for the supervising engineer. In 1832 Anderson was invited to render his account. Two years later, on his continuing failure to comply, the commissioners decided by majority vote to pay him three hundred guineas. The recipient, however, had not forgotten his experience of earlier days of underpaid literary toil. He considered this payment also totally inadequate. Stung perhaps by waspish criticism of additional expenditure on the project and of unnecessary ornamentation, for which he was not ultimately responsible, he retaliated with a voluminous report. This catalogued the effort required, including that generated by changes of plan during execution. He also drew attention to the system's additional capacity, the modest nature of his fee (as he saw it), and made no bones about the scale of his achievement. The town had been provided with pure and limpid water at all seasons, 'a task which no ordinary engineer could have undertaken, without the aid of a chemist.' To add insult to injury, his report and claim were mislaid during circulation among commission members. They surfaced two years later in the papers of Adam Pringle, a former lord provost. Anderson's claim was therefore re-submitted in January 1837 in even more vehement terms, coupled with the observation that he had 'frequently devoted, without the smallest pecuniary recompense, a large portion of my time to objects connected with the interests of the Community.' He saw no reason why his services should be less adequately compensated than those of a stranger, especially since local knowledge had been vital to success. Widespread approbation of the architecture and form of his creation had even extended to a request to send a description and sketch to the King of Prussia, through the Duchess of Cumberland, 'in order that a fac-simile [sic] of it might be erected in Berlin'. He reminded the commissioners that:

> Among the means that contribute to the cleanliness, health, and general comfort of all classes of society, there is none more essentially necessary than a regular, and abundant supply of pure and wholesome water.

The commission concurred, and, again by a majority, settled in full his claim for £850, a very substantial sum by contemporary standards.

The water system drew on a wide range of Anderson's skills - as chemist, physicist, geologist, mathematician, engineer, architect and politician - and his achievement was impressive. He foresaw the possibility of a population expansion and provided for additional demand of up to 50%. If required, a relatively inexpensive back-up reservoir could be constructed in the western suburbs, probably at Pomarium. The town's populace did increase, but its predicted spatial distribution was inaccurate. In the late nineteenth century physical settlement rose to altitudes that could no longer be serviced by the water level of the existing works. Consequently, new reservoirs were built further west and on higher ground than he anticipated. Designs to increase the head of water at the water works were produced in 1860, but proved abortive. Two years later a first reservoir was constructed at Wellshill; paradoxically this had been foreshadowed in a proposal of 1820 for a reservoir there. Additional reservoirs at Burghmuir and Viewlands were created in 1880, and these now supplied seventeen miles of piping.[24] The original water works building meantime, equipped with more engines, evolved as the pumping station for the entire system, which continued to provide the city's water until 1965, a total of 133 years. The water works were Anderson's most visible legacy and he derived lasting satisfaction from his success. Only a few days before his death in December 1846, he chalked the appropriate epitaph 'aquam igne et aqua haurio' (by fire and water I draw water) on the wall of the engine-room. Previously this whimsical preoccupation with classical inscriptions containing hidden nuances had been vented on the gas works, which he emblazoned with 'non fumam [sic — fumum?] ex fulgore sed ex fumo dare lucum' (literally meaning to produce, not smoke from flame, but light from smoke/fumes).[25]

It is testimony to Anderson's energy that, at the very height of the construction phase of Perth water works, he also found time to act as a consultant on a proposed water scheme for a second Perthshire community. The origins of this initiative are obscure, but by 1831 at the latest a committee had been appointed to consider the best mode of providing an adequate supply of clean water in Auchterarder. As in Perth, a rudimentary system based on wooden pipes already existed, but it too was inadequate. A half-mile walk down a steep brae was required and, in the words of a local organ, 'the business of a water carrier was no unprofitable trade'. Adam Anderson was commissioned to investigate options and make recommendations. His report, compiled in July 1831, noted that the 'inconveniences, and even privations' of a scanty or precarious supply were too obvious to require illustration. Had they not existed in Auchterarder, he observed, his report would not have been requested. Following this preamble, Anderson then documented his evaluation of four potential sources in terms of water quality, feasibility of supply, and engineering challenges, as well as capital and recurrent maintenance costs. Two sites were dismissed quickly: the Borewell was rejected owing to its hard water quality; whilst the Blindwell spring, unobjectionable in respect of water quality and adequacy of supply, was ruled out, because of its location. The latter lay nearly one hundred feet below the level of the town, making an effective supply at the point of use unachievable, even with sizeable investment in pumping apparatus and recurrent running costs.

Two realistic options remained. The first was a spring in the immediate vicinity of the head of the town. Using flow measurements recorded and transmitted by a Mr Syme, Anderson estimated that fully 10,000 gallons per day, or upwards of 50 Scots pints per family of six persons, would be available. He recommended the substitution of lead pipes (for wood), as at Perth, and the construction of a reservoir with a capacity of 1800 cubic feet at the most elevated point of the town. Technical and cost specifications for the engineering design and components were provided, with a prospective capital outlay of £200, and running costs of £10 per annum. Anderson's alternative site, the Cruccky [sic] Moss spring, southwest of the town, gave a significantly more prolific supply, which he estimated at 144,000 gallons per day. It was also of excellent quality, but involved 2,800 yards of piping as opposed to 800 yards. Capital and running costs were correspondingly higher: £695 and £35 respectively.[26] Action followed Anderson's report. At the instigation of Captain Marriott C. W. Aytoun of Glendevon, Royal Artillery, a water company was formed. In 1832, work commenced, and the defining features of Auchterarder's water system in Victorian times were laid: following Anderson's advice, a reservoir at Cruccky Moss [aka Crookie Moss, or Crook of Moss], fed a cistern near Townhead. This soon generated 72 gallons every minute, providing wholesome drinking water and permitting many individual houses to install baths - 'the water supplying not only the necessaries, but even the luxuries of life.' Only in January 1853 did the system temporarily succumb to unprecedented rain and floods, which burst part of the piping near the fountainhead. Aytoun had undertaken the leading role in engineering and financing the project, at a total cost of nearly £2,000. It was his scientific exertions, engineering skills, and 'generous heart', which were remembered as responsible for Auchterarder's water system. He was feted in April 1836, when an anniversary dinner was held, and subsequently given a lasting memorial when a public hall raised by public subscription was named after him.[27] Anderson's key contribution as consultant chemist and engineer to this second water scheme in Perthshire meantime slipped from sight, overshadowed in part by his contemporary achievement in Perth.

Although remembered chiefly for the Perth water works, however, his influence as engineering consultant touched many other spheres. Success bred renewed demands for his advice. Thus in 1833, when the Reverend James Esdaile complained of cold in the East

Church and requested council permission to install heating, his trump card was an intimation that Anderson had 'promised to apply his best skills to the subject and from the success which has attended all his other undertakings here and elsewhere ... we may fairly anticipate the most favorable [sic] result.' Added to the expectation that the congregation would require no financial subvention for the installation costs, the prospect of Anderson's involvement secured municipal blessing for any plan produced. Nevertheless, his advice was not invariably accepted. In 1836, for instance, the council received a complaint by Turnbull and Son, bleachers at Huntingtower, against operations by Sutherland of Pitcairnfield: the latter had filled up an old water course that acted as a safety valve for the Almond in flood. Anderson's plan for averting danger by cutting off a sluice to widen the main channel of the river and fill up the water track was rejected.

Of more significance however, Anderson was drawn into the vexed question of the town's river and rail communications. In the late 1820s the increasingly voluble and influential shipping interest was pushing its demand for improved navigation on the Tay to a belatedly successful conclusion, alarm at the implications for Perth's future as a port mounting with every addition to the harbour facilities at rival Dundee. One crucial concern was the proliferation of artificial hazards in the river as neighbouring landowners constructed fishing cairns, jetties and embankments to further salmon fishing or land reclamation schemes. To pre-empt possible litigation one of them, Sir John Richardson of Pitfour, invited the council in 1827 to inspect the site of a proposed new stone head at Cairney. Anderson and the burgh architect, William Mackenzie, were delegated to undertake the task and on receipt of their favourable report the council offered no opposition. Two years later Anderson again led a deputation downstream, which gave its blessing to a proposed embankment to be erected by Richardson and Allan of Errol. Perhaps these reports fed a reputation for impartiality since Thomas Mackay, factor to Sir David Moncreiffe, proposed in 1830 that Anderson should arbitrate in a dispute with the burgh architect over Moncreiffe's operations at the Weel ford, near Perth. If the arbitrator ratified Mackenzie's objections, Mackay engaged in advance to accept the outcome as binding.[28]

In 1832, two years after Perth's first navigation act had established a commission to promote a modest harbour improvement and remove the Weel ford, Anderson became embroiled once more. With Jardine and a party from the council he investigated potential and existing obstacles to shipping. The upshot was a recommendation that the Earl of Wemyss be allowed to join Sleepless Inch and Balhepburn Island with the mainland. It was hoped that improved scour would help to erode naturally impeding fords downstream from Friarton, since those had been excluded from the legally permissible operations of the commission. The deputation also condemned the proliferation of fishing cairns in the main stream and urged the removal of extended underwater jetties east of Newburgh. The far-reaching proposals embraced too a barrier of stones from the north bank to Mugdrum Island to divert tidal waves southwards and scour away sand deposits threatening Newburgh harbour's continuing role as Perth's outport. Anderson was, of course, personally very familiar with the Mugdrum stretch of the Tay, from both his family's coastal shipping activities and his earlier residence at Balgonie.

The deputation's recommendations set markers for the future activities of the navigation commission in straightening the river, narrowing its navigable channel, increasing its scour, and improving its shipping potential. Yet their short-term impact was limited. It took two years, following an influential report by the Stevensons, before the council gave tardy approval to the long-canvassed proposal to join Balhepburn with the mainland. Concurrently, the recommended junction of Mugdrum Island with the north bank was dropped from the second navigation bill after a local objection, since provision for it was not specifically included in the engineers' report. What Anderson and Jardine did accomplish was to focus attention on the limited value of the improvements embodied in the first navigation act of 1830, when carried out in isolation, leaving the numerous fords and other impedimenta downstream from Friarton untouched. Seven months later a council committee investigated the town's legal powers to deepen fords in the river's lower reaches and, after its encouraging observations, the Stevensons undertook a full survey of the Tay, a prelude to the more ambitious act of 1834. Meantime, disillusionment with the results of the earlier legislation grew, the luckless Jardine earmarked by some for the role of scapegoat; at a general meeting of the navigation commission in June 1833 his possible replacement was openly canvassed. The alternative favoured by one group was Anderson, whose triumph at the water works seemed in such marked contrast with Jardine's performance.

With the Stevensons enlisted as consultants to more comprehensive improvements, embracing the removal of fords as far as Newburgh and the construction of a tidal harbour, all encompassed in the new 1834 act, public opinion was placated and Anderson could divert his attention to a new issue. This emerged in 1835 when Lord Kinnaird first promoted seriously the idea of a railway line between Perth and Dundee. His engineer painted a seductive picture of the scheme releasing 'the cramped energies' of Perth's entrepreneurs and terminating an alleged flight of capital to Dundee. From the outset two problems appeared: a suitable site for the Perth terminus and a convenient crossing point on the river. At first the council was insistent that the station should be in Perth itself and in November 1835, after asking Anderson to inspect Kinnaird's proposed route to Barnhill in company with Mackenzie and the river superintendent, endorsed their opinion that the railway should cross the Tay near the water works and run into a terminus behind the site. Shipping would have continuing access upstream to Perth's ancient harbours at Old Shore and Coal Shore through the incorporation of a drawbridge in the railway bridge.[29] A few months later however, deadlock was reached when Kinnaird's counter-proposal for a crossing at Inchyra, with a swing bridge, threatened to jeopardise the substantial investment in recent navigational improvements and permit railways from the south to by-pass the town en route to Dundee and the north-east.

An hiatus followed, but the rail mania of 1844-45 revived the proposal for a bridge at Mugdrum. Dundee's powerful claims for direct communications with the south and cheap access to Fife's coal reserves to feed her industries appeared in irreconcilable conflict with Perth's stake in unimpeded river navigation. Panic mounted as vast sums had been sunk in the waterway by the 1840s, in addition to undertakings to recompense the salmon fishing proprietors for any losses, all on the security of the city's revenues. With the influential backing of the Admiralty, disturbed by the implications of the Mugdrum project for navigation in tidal estuaries throughout Britain, Perth succeeded in defeating the railway lobby.[30] A modified scheme for a wooden viaduct at the south tip of Moncreiffe Island, thereafter crossing the river channel 480 feet downstream from the water works, threatened to obliterate half the new docks and sever the town's communications with them. After advice from the Stevensons, the council also resisted this proposal successfully. Agreement was eventually reached with the Dundee and Perth Railway Company towards the close of 1846 to cross the Tay north of the water works at the site suggested by Anderson eleven years earlier. The concordat included too an undertaking by the company to carry out their operations under his direct sight and to his satisfaction.

This outcome was a peculiarly personal relief to Anderson: in the preceding year, as an interested neighbouring proprietor in his own right at St Leonard's Bank, he was one of several property owners who expressed outrage at the council's decision to sacrifice part of Perth's South Inch to accommodate a more central rail terminus. The proposal, by those he castigated as 'our present barbarous magistrates', split both council and community, and was finally reversed in Parliament. He lived to hear that verdict, but not to witness its implementation. When the agreement with the railway company was reported officially to the councillors, on 7 December 1846, the next item on their agenda was news of Anderson's death two days earlier. Initially a terminus was opened at Barnhill in June 1847, but two years later a wooden viaduct carried the line over the Tay, a swing bridge ensuring upstream movement for shipping. At a suitable height the line continued north of the water works to a station at Princes Street, in accord with Anderson's proposals, but this was soon extended to the new general terminus at St Leonard's.[31] With it the threat to the town's environment was removed: Scott's 'Fair City' would remain intact.

NOTES

1   PTC Min., 3 Sep., 5 Nov. 1821.

2   *ibid.*, 16 Sep. 1765, 1 Dec. 1766, 7 Dec. 1772, 20 Aug., 11 Oct. 1773, 19 Sep. 1778, 7 June 1779; G. Penny, *Traditions of Perth*, (Perth: Dewar [et al], 1836), 113.

3   PTC Min., 6 and 13 Oct. 1788, 5 Jan., 16 Mar. 1789, 3 Dec. 1792, 23 Aug., 7 Oct. 1793, 7 Apr. 1794, 6 July, 3 Aug. 1795, 3 July, 14 Aug. 1797, 7 Apr. 1800, 6 June, 1 Aug., 10 Oct. 1803, 2 Sep. 1805, 3 June 1811.

4   J. Maiben & Co., *Statement of the advantages to be derived from the introduction of coal gas into factories and dwelling houses*, (Perth, 1813); *Perth Courier*, 18 Oct., 6, 13 and 27 Dec. 1822; *Contract of co-partnery of the Perth Gas Light Company*, (Perth, [1823]), 3,11.

5   *Perth Courier*, 31 Dec. 1822, 24 Jan., 28 Feb., 7 Mar., 25 Apr., 16 May 1823, 15 Dec. 1825.

6   PTC Min., 5 May, 7 July 1823, 1 Nov. 1824; *Perth Courier*, 12 Sep. 1823, 6 and 27 Feb., 16 July, 15 Oct., 31 Dec. 1824, 21 Jan., 4 Feb., 11 Mar., 17 June, 11 Aug. 1825, 16 Feb. 1826; [Edinburgh:] N[ational] A[rchives of] S[cotland, HM General Register House], CH2/521/30.] P[erth] G[eneral] K[irk] S[ession] Min[utes], 2 Sep., 21 Oct. 1824.

7   PTC Min., 4 Feb., 7 Apr. 1828, 18 Dec. 1833, 24 Mar., 5 Sep., 15 Oct. 1836, 7 Aug. 1837, 5 Feb., 1 Oct. 1838; *Perth Courier*, 9 Aug., 15 Nov. 1827, 3 May 1832, 13 May 1841; G. Penny, *Statistical account of the city of Perth*, (Perth, 1842), 2.

8   *Perth Courier*, 4 and 11 Feb., 11 Mar. 1825, 20 Sep. 1827, 28 Oct. 1830.

9   *ibid.*, 18 Aug. 1825, 4 and 11 Sep., 9 Oct. 1828, 13 Oct. 1836; PTC Min., 6 May, 3 June 1844, 5 May, 2 June, 7 July, 1 Sep., 6 Oct., 3 Nov. 1845.

10 PTC Min., 1 Mar. 1824, 2 May, 5 Dec. 1825, 3 Apr., 1 May, 3 July, 4 Dec. 1826; *Perth Courier*, 3 Aug., 12 Oct. 1826.

11 A. Anderson, *Appendix to the report on the weights and measures of Perthshire*, (Perth: R. Morison, 1827), 1.

12 *Perth Courier*, 3 Apr., 8 May, 24 July, 7 and 14 Aug. 1828; PTC Corr., PE/430. A. Anderson to Lord Provost R. Ross, Perth, 7 May 1828.

13 PTC Min., 16 Oct. 1752, 2 Apr. 1759, 19 Apr., 10 Nov. 1762, 4 Feb., 5 Aug., 2 Sep. 1765, 31 Mar. 1766, 11 Sep. 1786, 2 and 16 Mar. 1789, 1 Feb., 5 Apr. 1790, 2 Apr., 7 May 1792, 1 Aug., 5 Sep. 1796, 1 May, 14 Aug. 1797.

14 *ibid.*, 3 Aug. 1772, 3 Feb., 30 June 1777, 4 Apr. 1785, 5 June 1786, 1 June 1789, 6 June, 4 July 1791, 1 May 1797, 6 May, 3 June 1799, 2 Sep. 1805, 4 Dec. 1809, 4 June 1810, 2 Mar. 1812, 3 Jan. 1814, 3 Apr., 5 June 1815.

15 *Perth Courier*, 14 May 1818, 29 Mar. 1822, 23 Nov. 1826.

16 *ibid.*, 30 June, 11 Aug. 1814, 9 and 23 Mar. 1815; PTC Min., 8 Nov. 1781, 6 June, 4 July 1785, 8 Oct., 3 Dec. 1787, 6 July 1795, 6 Aug. 1804, 4 Nov. 1805, 11 Jan., 1 Aug., 5 Sep. 1808, 3 Apr., 5 June 1815, 1 Jan. 1827.

17 *ibid.*, 3 May, 6 Sep. 1819, 3 Apr. 1820, 26 Jan. 1823, 2 June 1828; *Perth Courier*, 29 July 1819, 22 Nov. 1822.

18 [Perth: Perth & Kinross Archives at A K Bell Library.] P[erth] W[ater] C[ommission] Min[utes], 28 June 1837 [Report to the commission by Adam Anderson].

19 *ibid.*, 28 June 1837; PTC Min., 3 Feb. 1823, 5 Mar., 6 Aug. 1827, 6 Oct. 1828; *Perth Courier*, 4 June 1822, 13 Oct., 22 Dec. 1825, 29 Mar., 6 Sep. 1827.

20 *ibid.*, 31 Jan., 7 Aug., 6 and 13 Nov., 4 Dec. 1828, 12 and 19 Mar. 1829, 7 and 14 Jan. 1830; PWC Min., 28 June 1837; PTC Min., 29 Dec. 1829, 15 Feb. 1830.

21 *Perth Courier*, 11 Dec. 1828, 8 and 21 Jan., 12 Feb., 12 and 26 Mar., 28 May, 11 June, 17 Sep., 31 Dec. 1829.

22 *ibid.*, 29 Oct. 1829, 25 Mar., 19 Aug. 1830; PWC Min., 8 June, 20 Oct., 21 and 26 Dec. 1829, 17 Feb., 20 Mar. 1830; PTC Min., 29 Dec. 1829, 15 Feb. 1830.

[23] *ibid.*, 10 June, 10, 21 and 30 Aug. 1830, 21 Feb., 31 Mar., 12 Apr.,
5 and 7 May, 27 Dec. 1831, 20 Sep., 15 Nov. 1832, 3 Apr. 1833, 31
Aug. 1835, 28 June 1837; *Perth Courier*, 21 Oct. 1830; *N[ew]
S[tatistical] A[ccount of Scotland]*, (Edinburgh: Blackwood & Sons,
1845), vol. x, Perthshire, parish of Perth, 86.

[24] PWC Min., 28 June 1837; PTC Min., 7 Feb. 1820; F. Groome:
Ordnance Gazeteer of Scotland, 6 vols., (Edinburgh: T. & C. Jack,
1882-85), vol. 1, 182.

[25] *Auld Perth;* ed. by A.R. Urquhart, (Perth: J. McGregor, 1906), 25;
D. Peacock, *Perth: its annals and its archives*, (Perth: T.
Richardson, 1849), 501; *In memoriam* (reprinted from the *Perth
Courier*), 1867, 1-3.

[26] A. Anderson: *Report respecting the most eligible mode of supplying
the town of Auchterarder with water*, (xerox copy of Anderson's
report, dated 21 July 1831, Perth, in author's possession.)

[27] Alexander G. Reid: *The Annals of Auchterarder and memorials of
Strathearn*, (Crieff: David Philips, 1899), 299; *NSA*, vol. x,
Perthshire, parish of Auchterarder, 296-97; *Perthshire
Constitutional*, 6 Apr. 1836; *Perthshire Courier*, 6 Jan. 1853;
'Aytoun Hall – its past and future ?', *Auchterarder Local History
Newsletter*, 10 (spring 2005), 3

[28] PTC Min., 4 and 14 June 1827, 1 June, 6 July 1829, 4 Jan. 1830, 4
Feb. 1833, 11 June 1836.

[29] *ibid.*, 3 Dec. 1821, 7 May, 3 Dec. 1832, 4 Feb., 4 Mar., 1 July 1833,
27 Jan., 17 Mar. 1834, 2, 9, 12 and 17 Nov. 1835; *Perth Courier*, 20
June 1833, 19 Nov. 1835; *NSA*, vol. x, Perthshire, parish of Perth,
102-3; J.R. Findlater, *Report relative to the formation of a railway
between the towns of Dundee and Perth*, (Dundee, 1835), 6-9.

[30] PTC Min., 1 Feb., 4 Apr., 2 May, 6 June 1836, 1 Apr., 18 Sep., 7
Oct. 1844, 7 Apr. 1845; Tidal Harbours Commission, *Second
report*, 179-93.

[31] PTC Min., 8 May 1845, 7 Dec. 1846; D. Peacock, *op. cit.*, 576;
Perth Academy. [xerox copy]. A. Anderson to Andrew
Anderson, jun., [son], Croft [Perth], 15 Sep. 1845.

KINCARDINE PIER

Plate 1: Kincardine-on-Forth in the nineteenth century: its vibrant shipping activities, and his family's deep involvement in them, were significant formative influences on the young Adam Anderson.

Plate 2: Old Tulliallan Churchyard, Kincardine-on-Forth. Several gravestones display symbols reflecting the importance of Kincardine's shipping interests. The Anderson family stone carries an anchor and sextant.

Plate 3: Portrait of Adam Anderson by Thomas Duncan, RSA. *Courtesy of St Andrews University Museum Collections.*

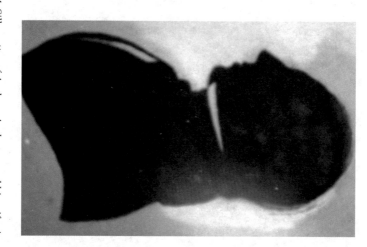

Plate 4: Silhouettes of Andrew Anderson and his wife, Agnes Anderson (nee Ramsay). Their marriage in 1815, a true love match, also confirmed Anderson's acceptance by the city's social elite. *Courtesy of Mr P Nicholson & Mrs L Kavanagh.*

Plate 5: Silhouette of James Ramsay of Croft, Lord Provost of Perth in 1794-96, father-in-law to Adam Anderson, a leading member of the city's privileged political elite prior to municipal reform. *Courtesy of Mr P Nicholson & Mrs L Kavanagh.*

Plate 6: The Croft, also known as Croft House, the residence of the Ramsay family. In the 1840s, on vacation from St Andrews University, a garret room once served Anderson as his 'workshop, library, w.c....as variously furnished as Noah's Ark'. The house, altered later in the 19th century, no longer stands.

76

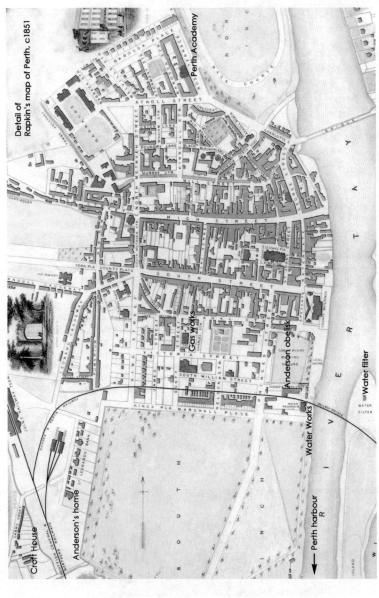

Detail of
Rapkin's map of Perth, c1851

Perth Academy

Gas Works

Anderson obelisk

Croft House

Anderson's home

Water Works

Perth harbour

Water filter

Plate 7: Perth in 1851. Note the proximity of the water filter in Moncreiffe Island to the water works in Marshall Place. *Courtesy of Perth & Kinross Archives.*

Plate 8: Perth Academy, Rose Terrace, photographed by A Mackenzie, from the Wood Collection. This image shows the exterior of the school in the third quarter of the 19th century, when comparatively little had changed since Anderson's time as rector, between 1809 and 1837. Note the absence of later accretions, such as the statue of Britannia. *Courtesy of Perth Museum.*

Plate 9: Elevation of the Reservoir for Supplying the City of Perth with water [drawn by Adam Anderson]. *Courtesy of Dundee Central Library, Local History Centre.*

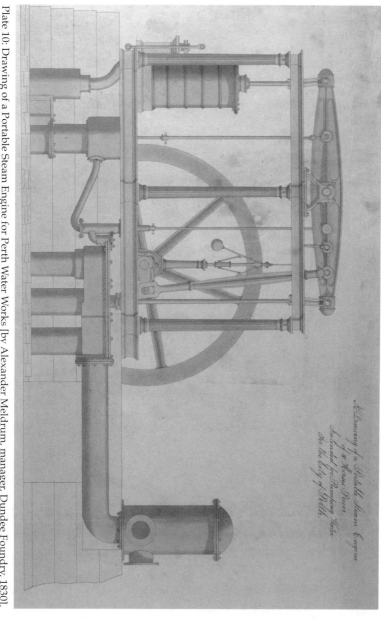

Plate 10: Drawing of a Portable Steam Engine for Perth Water Works [by Alexander Meldrum, manager, Dundee Foundry, 1830].
Courtesy of Dundee Central Library, Local History Centre.

Plate 11: The South Inch overlooked by St Leonard's Bank, from the photographic studio of Magnus Jackson, in the late nineteenth century. Anderson's house is on the far left. His intervention helped to prevent the construction of Perth's railway station in the park, thus saving the 'city feel' that owes so much to the clear vistas of Perth's Georgian terraces. *Courtesy of Perth Museum.*

Plate 12: Adam Anderson's house at St Leonard's Bank, overlooking the South Inch, was his second residence there. On a double feu purchased from the Glover Incorporation in 1830, strict conditions required him to erect a mansion of high quality and a value of at least £800.

Plate 13: Thomas Chalmers (1780-1847), leading Evangelical in the Scottish Kirk, first Moderator of the Free Kirk after the Disruption, and arguably the most influential mover of Scots middle-class opinion, was a lifelong friend of Anderson from their student days at St Andrews. *Courtesy of University of St Andrews Library.*

Plate 14: Sir David Brewster (1781-1868), Principal of United College from 1838, was a giant of Scottish science, notably in optics. A supportive referee and another lifelong acquaintance of Anderson, Brewster's career had many similarities, but his irascible temperament and a vendetta against the aging Anderson in the Disruption era may have contributed to the latter's death. *Courtesy of University of St Andrews Library.*

Plate 15: St Salvator's Quadrangle, United College, St Andrews, c. 1849. Anderson's classroom occupied the upper storey of the building on the right. Despite its early morning smoke-filled interior, it became a legal and, on one occasion, physical battleground between Anderson and Brewster in the Principal's turf wars with the professoriate. *Courtesy of University of St Andrews Library.*

Plate 16: Obelisk in GreyFriars Burying Ground, Perth, erected to the memory of Adam Anderson following a public appeal for funds in 1867. The inscription states: 'This monument is erected by some of his friends and former pupils in testimony of their admiration of his high scientific attainments and great moral worth.'.

5

HEALING MEASURES: POLITICS, THE GREAT REFORM ACT AND AFTER

As both teacher and engineer Adam Anderson personified two dominant themes of his time: the quantum leap of science and technology and the increasing importance of the urban middle classes. Yet these were merely aspects of a kaleidoscope of contemporary change. In economic, social, political and religious terms, the late eighteenth and early nineteenth centuries were an age of revolutions. Although the apparent initial winners in terms of economic advancement and social status were the middle classes, they were not allowed to inherit free from anxiety. Many assumptions, in respect of the unique justice of their claim to political power for example, were challenged by a no longer silent majority, some of whom were either casualties of economic change or whose expectations were raised by it. Perth was hardly a sprouting mushroom of the Industrial Revolution, despite some misleading symptoms of commercial promise in the mid-eighteenth century. Yet, as a textile centre with a population of 20,016 by 1831, it could not escape the sharpening of social division and the importation of new political philosophies that recognised neither burghal nor national boundaries. Though in many respects an archetypal representative of the new successful middle-class professional, Anderson was also a polymath whose breadth of vision grasped more clearly than most contemporaries the implications of the metamorphosis that was taking place around him. His response to prevailing social and political dislocation reflected the interaction of these influences on him.

Not all the new forces seemed cast from the outset in an inevitably destabilising role. The same year Anderson left St

Andrews, William Paley published his influential *Natural theology; or, evidences of the existence of the Deity, collected from the appearances of nature*. Far from being an attack on the rise of modern science as a threat to religion, it deployed scientific empiricism and mechanism to buttress existing belief. In the early nineteenth century science and religion were not just in harmony but also mutually interdependent. As scientists explored nature in deep awe of an unfolding Divine design, theologians eagerly grasped new scientific discoveries as additional evidence of the Creator's hand. Darwinism, with its alternative hypothesis of functional adaptations through genetic selection and without reference to a Designer, lay in the future;[1] *The Origin of species* was published thirteen years after Anderson's death. Nonetheless, the profusion and direction of scientific enquiry already caused mounting unease among some theologians. With the cork out of the bottle, there was no guarantee that the contents could be contained.

Like Paley, Thomas Chalmers was an amateur scientist: in 1815 his Kilmany manse carried scars of attempts at installing rudimentary gas lighting.[2] Anderson also, as observed, shared with the latter and Paley a perception of religion and science as twin facets of the search for Divine truth. But, if Chalmers in his student days had been no fundamentalist in his attitude towards aspects of Scripture, twenty years later his approach was more rigid. Both continued to espouse natural theology, but a difference in emphasis remained as each followed his own vocation. By 1818, Anderson felt compelled to defend the precedence he gave to scientific pursuits. He agreed with Chalmers:

> That every [d]escription of Science is nearly useless, unless it [is] made to bear on some shape or other upon the concerns of Eternity - and not only do I think so, but I uniformly labour to impress my convictions upon all over whom I have any influence. At the same time, I consider it my duty not only to give to the world such

discoveries as <u>may cast up</u> [Anderson's underlining] in the course of my professional labours, but to exert myself to the utmost of my abilities in expiscating new facts - and convinced as I am that all our discoveries, whether in the moral or material world will ultimately promote the glory of the Great Creator, & the good of his creatures.

Along with this optimistic view he pointed out to Chalmers the necessity of promoting as teachers those who combined 'a pious cast of mind' with a scientific outlook. Both clergy and laity, he alleged, had failed in this respect in the past, abandoning youth 'to receive such Instructions, as chance may throw in their way'.[3]

Anderson continued to keep Chalmers abreast of his latest scientific enquiries. The cleric would once have taken considerable interest in them, but Anderson appreciated that his attention was 'now devoted to more important objects'. He could only hope that Chalmers would not dismiss them as 'useless'.[4] In fact, Chalmers never totally forfeited an interest in science, even on the eve of the Disruption of the Scottish Kirk. In autumn 1840, he engaged Anderson to accompany him in giving fund-raising lectures on the properties of heat at the opening of a new mechanics' institute in Greenock. Yet the differing emphasis remained: Chalmers' mission there was 'to protest against any system which would dissociate religion from scholarship' and, although scientific experiments dominated the course, his 'special office' was clear; that was:

Not only to point out the theology that might be educed [sic] from the glories of the divine workmanship, but, if possible, to neutralise the mischief that flows from but a little learning — when unaccompanied with certain principles and considerations.

By contrast, Anderson enthusiastically promoted science for its own sake, whatever risks might accrue from partial knowledge, though adding as an important corollary that 'he was particularly desirous to impress ... the necessity of an unceasing recognition of the hand of God in all of his works, and the still higher duty of submitting themselves to the glorious discoveries of revelation.' Like Chalmers therefore, he recognised dangers as well as opportunities where so many were, in Lord Cockburn's words, 'nibbling at the teats of science'. Later, as a professor at St Andrews, Anderson would impress on his students that there was 'a Great First Cause who brought all things into being, encouraging them to look 'from nature to nature's God'.[5]

If religious belief in his lifetime felt merely the early tremors of the forthcoming Darwinian volcano, the institution of the church in Scotland was subjected to a more immediate onslaught and ultimately shattered by a crisis with roots embedded in the early eighteenth century. Contrary to the provisions of the Act of Union, lay patronage had been restored in 1712, effectively reinstating the selection of the parish ministry as a property right of local landowners. With the congregational 'call' becoming in time an empty formality, resistance to patronage mounted, leading to repeated secessions from the Established Kirk. When the 'new light' of voluntaryism, or separation from state endowment, became the adopted ideal of many seceders for church-state relations, dissent emerged in the early nineteenth century as a formidable opposition to the Church of Scotland, particularly in new, unchurched, urban communities. In turn, within the Established Kirk, opinion polarised on how to meet the challenge. By then the dominant Moderate party identified with the landed interest to the extent of accepting patronage as a positive good, rather than merely unavoidable. The Evangelical party likewise changed, forsaking strict Calvinist exclusiveness for the promotion of 'mission' at home and abroad, not least as a counter to seceder advances in the industrial conurbations. Attaining power in the general assemblies of the 1830s, the Evangelicals attempted to circumvent the rights of lay patrons through a qualified congregational veto on unacceptable nominees. The resulting collision between clerical and civil jurisdictions was exacerbated by deep-seated political and social attitudes on both sides and a grim determination to disdain compromise. The 'Ten Years' Conflict' climaxed in 1843, with the largest secession of all, dividing the mainstream of the Scottish Kirk for nearly ninety years.

Even more than natural theology these highly emotive, divisive issues forced adherents of the Church of Scotland to take sides; Adam Anderson was no exception. Although science triumphed over religion in the battle for his career choice, he remained, as noted earlier, a devout Christian throughout life. Within the Established Kirk he was moreover a lay activist for most of it, ordained deacon two years after his arrival in Perth and elder in 1818.[6] He was involved in evangelising Christian bodies too. Indeed, his address to the Perthshire Bible Society in 1821, on 'the duty of contributing to the dissemination of the scriptures', was later published in pamphlet form.[7] Six years on he twisted Chalmers' arm to come and inject the languishing Perthshire Missionary Society with new life, since it promoted 'a cause which you have too much at heart not to embrace every opportunity of fostering & encouraging.'[8] As an elder, however, his principal personal contribution was made within the congregation of the conservative Dr James Esdaile and the town's East Kirk. Though its parish included the socially deprived weaver suburb of Pomarium, it recruited mainly the social elite of Perth and its immediate rural vicinity. With few exceptions they followed their pastor, despite his support for the Evangelicals' Veto Act of 1834, in remaining loyal to the state church at the Disruption.

Anderson was likewise a staunch upholder of the establishment principle. In 1834, as the voluntaryist challenge became acute, his sympathies were made clear and public. Toasting 'church and state' at a dinner to honour Esdaile's pamphleteering assaults on dissenters, Anderson launched an uncharacteristically bitter attack on those with whom he disagreed. Re-connecting with the strong animus against religious sectarians, which he had developed in his student days, he accused voluntaries of trying to 'divest' states of their Christian character and of not hesitating 'to league themselves with the infidel and the scoffer'. Three years later, when the Whigs, under dissenter pressure, proposed to abolish church rates south of the Border, threatening maintenance of the fabric of the Church of England, he openly associated himself with those concerned at the implications for the establishment principle in general.[9] Anderson also served on a committee of the Kirk's general session in Perth set up to found a library 'principally of Religious publications to circulate among the people belonging to the Establishment.' Its objective was to strengthen the argumentative resources of the state church in the battle with dissent. Paradoxically, despite such forays into the minefield of ecclesiastical politics, his perceived detachment was still sufficient to be allotted the delicate task of toasting 'clergy of all denominations' at a civic banquet during the royal visit to Perth in 1842.[10]

In the run-up to the Disruption Anderson maintained a low profile on the growing divisions within the Established Kirk and his attitudes are barely discernible. An initial identification with Chalmers may, unsurprisingly, be adduced. In 1827 he looked forward to the latter's translation to the divinity chair at Edinburgh, in which:

> The country is likely to reap the benefit of your labours, in a field of such extreme usefulness ... The prospect of that event, which has been long wished for, not only by your friends, but by every sincere well-wisher of the Church, has given to every person the greatest satisfaction, with the exception of the few party-spirited individuals who would sacrifice every consideration to their own selfish views.[11]

Hostile to all sectarianism, he was neither a Moderate nor Evangelical partisan. Some latent sympathy with the general outlook of the Evangelicals within the Kirk nonetheless may be inferred from requests to Chalmers to use influence on behalf of specific candidates for clerical vacancies. Thus Anderson pled James Gray's claims to Gask in 1828 on his 'truly evangelical spirit' and adherence to 'all the great doctrines for which you yourself [Chalmers] have so successfully contended'. Likewise, Esdaile's son had views on theology, which were 'scriptural and consistent, and, of course, *evangelical* in the popular acceptation of the phrase.'[12] In the event, David Esdaile, like his father, remained within the Established Kirk in 1843. Anderson too declined to follow Chalmers into the Free Kirk: his memorial service was to be conducted by Esdaile's successor in the Established East Church. Underlying sympathy with the missionary commitment of the Evangelicals stopped far short, of endorsing any messianic drive to secession. That degree of enthusiasm, extremism and partisanship was alien to Anderson's nature. He was dismayed when the zeal of Candlish and young hardliners of the 'wild party' led to sectarianism, bitterness and schism, replicating all too closely, in his eyes, the intolerance of Dissent.

In politics too moderation and the middle ground were Anderson's watchwords. As a student, he had witnessed personally the impact of nepotism and corruption under the ancien regime, and had vented his feelings on its most prominent proponent in St Andrews, Dr Hill. He was likewise incensed at the university's 'very servile' address, signed by the principal, to Viscount Melville on his acquittal in 1806. Melville's friends had no reason to celebrate a triumph, he felt, since he had merely escaped 'by the partial decision of the Judges, all of whom except one were nominated to office by Mr Pitt and himself, and of course were naturally disposed to put the most favourable construction on his conduct'. Anderson had no doubt that Melville had misapplied the £10,000, with which he was charged, for the purpose of bribery.[13] This disillusionment with the judiciary and Pitt marked a shift in attitudes. The previous year he had given tacit support to Pitt personally, even if already disenchanted with the prime minister's ministry:

> This country stands in a very critical situation – Public corruption, & public mismanagement will do us more harm than all the attempts of our Enemies – All

> Mr Pitt's measures have proved ineffectual
> since his last restoration to office, and
> indeed how can it be otherwise, when he is
> distracted by examinations, with scarcely a
> man of any abilities in Administration to
> give him advice, or support.[14]

Progressive influences on him inevitably strengthened, when he joined the Greenhills. The family was of Whig persuasion, through which Anderson rubbed shoulders with ascending figures of the same faith, notably the Maules and Adam (later Lord) Gillies.[15] The contrast with the atmosphere of Dundas Toryism pervading St Andrews under Principal Hill must have been stark. Though exposed to Whig reforming ideals at Fern, their durability was to be tested nonetheless after his move to Perth.

On arrival in the city he was careful, as always, to nurture an image of impeccable respectability, concealing anything that could threaten his standing. When his young sister and a friend proposed to visit him a few months after his appointment to the academy, Anderson arranged to meet and collect them at Bridge of Earn, since 'it would not look well for them to come to the very door in a cart'. Following his appointment to Perth Academy, as a bachelor of twenty-nine, thoughts of marriage, encouraged by the presence of 'plenty of good-looking & well-tochered lasses', again populated correspondence to his parents.[16] Six years later, his dual search for a wife and a wealthy connection, was eventually fulfilled. On 31 July 1815, after a courtship of at least two years, and despite a broken engagement, commemorated by Anderson personally in poetry and in carving on a heart-shaped wooden box, he married Agnes Ramsay.[17] Through her he entered one of Perth's privileged ancien regime families, sole repositories of political influence before the parliamentary and municipal reform legislation of the 1830s. His father-in-law, James Ramsay of Croft, had been lord provost in 1794-96, a period when local Radical enthusiasm for the French Revolution prompted the government commander-in-chief in Scotland, Lord Adam Gordon, to describe Perth as 'a very dangerous place'.

Exertions in maintaining tranquility in the burgh had earned Ramsay the coveted approbation of the Duke of Athole.[18] Eleven years after their marriage however, Agnes died, leaving Anderson with sole responsibility for raising their young family of three daughters — Eliza, Amelia Agnes and Jemima - and one son, Andrew. A few years after this event Anderson, already resident in St Leonard's Bank, purchased a double plot from the Glover Incorporation in the same locality. Overlooking the South Inch, his new mansion, constructed to exacting standards, and at great cost, made him the immediate neighbour of his in-laws. If anything his bond with the Ramsays grew stronger: towards the end of his life he let his own house and moved into their rather overcrowded accommodation at the Croft.[19]

Combined with a growing scientific reputation and moral stature, the Ramsay connection confirmed his acceptance into Perth's social elite. As a leading pillar of the middle-classes, he played a prominent role in the town's social life, from the Royal Golfing Society, of which he was a founder and council member, to the Perth assemblies, in which he acted as joint director. Invariably, his name appeared in subscription lists for public objects, while he was in constant demand at communal events.[20] Yet, he could never be wholly absorbed into the city's manufacturing and commercial circles. While sharing many of their anxieties and attitudes, his intellect and scholarship endowed him with greater capacity to place them in context and to articulate them. Relative detachment and unflagging energy elevated him in many eyes as a potentially valuable ally to mobilise support for political and social palliatives. Sufficiently representative of the substantial middle-classes, with whom he mingled, to be concerned in particular about the challenge of political radicalism, his own antidotes were applied social concern and moderate constitutional reform.

Traditional social welfare provision through kirk sessions, aimed at the relief of occasional and limited distress, demonstrably failed by the early nineteenth century to cope with demands generated by new economic conditions. Slumps in an industrialised society produced mass unemployment on a previously unparalleled scale. Subscriptions to provide relief became commonplace and Anderson, like most individuals of his social level, regularly responded to appeals for aid. His selection, together with the Middle Kirk minister, to distribute substantial amounts of meal and coal donated to the poor by Lord Gray of Kinfauns during the 1831-32 depression, reflected both his public standing and a long personal association with the peer. Additionally by then, his concern for the underprivileged was well known. Less than two years after his arrival in Perth he was lecturing on behalf of philanthropic causes. In due course the proceeds of public lectures on chemistry and similar topics helped to augment the resources of a variety of bodies, such as the Ladies Charitable Society, the Destitute Sick Society and the Auxiliary Deaf and Dumb Society.[21]

In the absence of legal provision for medical care, participation in voluntary organisations and fund-raising was a normal middle-class preoccupation. The scope and incentive for health prevention measures dramatically increased however, with the onset of cholera in 1832. Confronted with this crisis an essentially eighteenth-century local government system was demonstrably inadequate. As the death toll mounted, a representative, voluntary board of health was formed and Anderson became a member. By April over 31,000 quarts of soup and 32,000 loaves of bread had been distributed in an attempt to shore up the nutritional defences of the most impoverished sections of society. This drive to strengthen their resistance, added to extraordinary sanitary measures, greatly lessened the lethal impact of the epidemic in the burgh. Anderson's involvement in the battle against cholera and other infectious diseases continued nonetheless beyond the immediate panic. He remained on the local dispensary committee and emerged prominently again when this in turn gave ground to more ambitious schemes for public health. On 5 October 1836, the foundation stone was laid of Perth's first city and county infirmary; Anderson was charged with organising the inaugural procession that snaked along a tortuous route from the river to the construction site west of the city centre.

In a complex motivation for these activities, theoretical and financial objections to the alternative of compulsory assessments were certainly factors. Added to his own hard-headed approach to money, he shared the strong views of Thomas Chalmers on the necessity of voluntary giving as an essential manifestation of the Calvinist social conscience. 'All legal provisions for the poor', Anderson wrote, were 'not only encroachments upon the province of Christian charity but so many inducements to indolence, thoughtless extravagance, & insubordination.'.[22] Though reflecting contemporary middle-class preoccupations, that 'the poor' had to be prevented from sliding into an immoral dependence on charity, he could still entertain genuine concern for the victims of ill health or economic disaster. In words he used to describe an acquaintance, he was himself 'a friend to every philanthropic Institution in this town'.[23]

His attachment, with reservations, to the ecclesiastical *status quo* was paralleled by a similar qualified fidelity to its secular counterpart. Although his rectorial appointment had been supported by the influence of Greenhill and his allies, and he had rubbed shoulders for years with the Whig elite of Angus, Anderson's marriage placed him firmly within one of Perth's privileged ruling families. His first public step into the political arena after his marriage suggested that, probably influenced by his marital connections, his attachment to the existing constitutional order had grown. The occasion was proposed government legislation to deprive Queen Caroline of her title following the accession of her husband, George IV. The characters of both monarchs and the circumstances of their marriage rendered the queen an equivocal symbol of resistance to ministerial oppression, but Anderson's open identification with the conservative side of this *cause célèbre* was revealing. When the local Guildry gave support to the queen in autumn 1820, he emerged as one of seventy-four prominent Perth citizens who protested at the incorporation's action as 'implying a doubt of the justice and integrity of one of the Supreme Branches of the Legislature.' While some Whigs signed this protest, the ringleaders were Tory members of the traditional ruling classes, like Robert Ross of Oakbank. In a critic's words, they were a minority who preponderated in 'mere wealth'.[24]

Anderson's friend, Esdaile, admittedly engaged later in an attempt to clear the rector's name of imputations that he was a radical Liberal, also stressed the underlying conservatism of his political outlook. He recalled that after Anderson's arrival, he was a decided supporter of Pitt's administration, writing weekly in its defence in the *Perth Courier*, 'of which he was the conductor'.[25] Pitt the Younger had died before Anderson's coming to Perth, but an empathy with the former and his espousal of limited, practical reform was manifested in Anderson's early correspondence. Less plausible is Esdaile's implication that Anderson acted as editor of the local liberal Tory organ published by the Morison family. Anything as formal and time-consuming, even in early nineteenth-century terms, would have contravened the spirit and letter of his appointment at Perth Academy, but he possibly contributed regular anonymous leaders. Certainly he published in its columns during the 1819-20 'Radical War'. Lord Gray later recalled that Anderson had 'on all occasions been a staunch friend and supporter of the Government and ... by his writings in the *Perth Courier*, and other personal exertions has been greatly the means of preventing any radical meeting from taking place in this neighbourhood'.[26] By 1820, the pivot of radicalism had switched from the east of Scotland to the newly-industrialised west, so his role was perhaps overstated, but Gray at least confirmed Anderson's reputation as a quiet but effective defender of the existing political order.

Rejected by Edinburgh's pre-reform city council electorate in 1831 the Whig lord advocate, Francis Jeffrey, sought entry to Parliament through the Forfar district of burghs, which included Perth. Against a backcloth of reform fever and widespread demonstrations, the Perth councillors agreed, with only two abstentions, to support him. The usual celebratory dinner attracted 350 guests of all political shades, including Anderson as a croupier. His toast to the Scottish bar alluded to Jeffrey's 'enlightened views, the high literary reputation, and to the splendid and varied talents of a man, whose name is so clearly interwoven with the literature, and the science, and the general improvement of the age in which we live'. This personal, almost apolitical tribute allowed Esdaile to contend subsequently that Anderson had been 'induced ... by the influence of his former Whig friends, to attend at the Dinner ... and from that moment he has been constantly plied by that Party on account of the weight which they conceived his name and respectability would give to their cause.'[27]

Conservatives as well as Whigs saw Anderson, however, as a potential asset during the reform struggle. In April 1831 they had witnessed the alarming spectacle of 6-7,000 people congregated in the short length of Perth's St John Street; disturbingly ordered and well-regulated demonstrators, 'walking arm in arm, six abreast, and comprising all the manufacturing population, from sprightly youth to tattering old age', had marched behind the blue blanket in support of the Reform Bill. Sir Alexander Muir Mackenzie of Delvine was one of those who sniffed revolution in the air and hoped that 'the respectable class of reformers' would condemn what he saw as violence and intimidation by political unions and sedition by the fourth estate. In particular, 'if a person so much respected as Dr Anderson, for instance, would take that line; he might do much good', and he might be persuaded 'to write some healing paper, & get it into the Perth & Strathmore Journal' (the local Liberal newspaper founded in Coupar Angus as *The Strathmore Journal* but renamed later *The Perthshire Advertiser* after its migration to Perth). To Mackenzie, Anderson fitted the need for 'some respectable man in Perth; who tho' friendly to the measure of reform, in general — see that matters are carried too far; and that the populace is too much called into action.'[28] Whether Lord Provost Patrick Gilbert Stewart acted upon this suggestion and prevailed upon Anderson to put pen to paper is uncertain, but clearly by 1831 the latter was identifiable as a believer in an installment of constitutional change as necessary to preclude more radical alternatives.

The philosophy of flexible and regulated response from above was emphasised by Anderson at a reform rally on the South Inch, Perth, in May 1832, when he proposed resolutions conceding that reform had 'become absolutely necessary for the safety of the state'. Only days before, he had organised a display of waterworks and fireworks to salute the King's birthday; now he was obliged to argue that the monarch had been misled by unsound advice, but would come round to an appreciation of reality. His call for three cheers for reform was warmly greeted, but an attempt to raise a similar ovation for the sovereign drew a mixed response. Three months later the passage of reform was marked by celebrations which included an 'hydraulic exhibition' by Anderson in the town centre. This consisted of four dolphins spouting jets of water, which set wheels in motion, all appropriately embellished with reform slogans. Shorn of the latter ten years later, it would entertain Queen Victoria during her visit to Perth.[29] Meantime, the legislation of 1831-32, had two consequences locally. First, the town acquired its own member of parliament instead of sharing with Dundee, Forfar, Cupar and St Andrews. Secondly, the councillors lost their exclusive franchise to a new middle-class electorate of nearly eight hundred property-owners. But Anderson's remarkable political involvement in effectively helping to undermine his own employers' privileges did not end with the Reform Act.

In the first post-reform election Tory contenders, like John Richardson of Pitfour, appeared early in the field but retired through lack of support. Ironically, Perth's dominant Whig grandees had difficulty in finding a suitable candidate, leaving the election unexpectedly open. Lacking their own nominee, Conservatives faced a dilemma. They could support Lord James Stuart, former M.P. for Cardiff, who was approved by the Scottish Whig leadership popularly identified with the legal profession centred on Edinburgh's Parliament House. Alternately, they could opt for a more radical, but independent Whig, Laurence Oliphant of Condie, a man with local roots. Most chose Oliphant, determined to 'save the City from the fangs of the "Edinburgh Rump"', and forged in the process an unlikely alliance with local Radicals. Oliphant's coalition even embraced the non-voting working classes who already felt discarded by their former Whig associates of the reform agitation. The re-alignment was cemented by Oliphant's promise of moderate reform of the 'Bread Tax', or Corn Laws, 'that most important of all questions to the working classes'. This contrasted with Stuart's silence on the issue during fourteen years in Parliament.

Proposing Oliphant at the hustings Anderson pressed his claims, 'from his acquaintance with the principles of government, of business, manufactures and the arts, and his knowledge of the constituency, their wishes and their wants.' This was commendation of an individual, rather than a programme or party and, significantly, Oliphant's seconder, a local physician, was another stranger to the political limelight. This wide base of support, assured a landslide by 405 to 205 votes. Presiding over the inevitable victory dinner Anderson revealed a long personal acquaintance with the new MP and expressed confidence that he would try 'to do away with every real existing abuse of which the country had to complain'. Any impression that Anderson was fundamentally apolitical, and had naively been seduced into waters beyond his depth, would soon be dispelled. The following year his credentials as a long-standing political reformer were publicly confessed. Outlining the genesis of his principles, he recalled an early perception of 'the imperfections of the existing system of representation, in the flagrant abuses and gross corruption to which it gave birth'. Sheridan, Erskine and Fox had been early mentors, but it was Gray who had carried 'a more efficient and comprehensive system of Parliamentary Reform... It is this great healing measure – this measure of truly conservative policy', to which his fame would be owed. Here was the philosophy of principled, but conservative liberalism, in short of Whiggery and a stitch in time, the middle ground consensus that carried the Reform Act. In Anderson's hands it carried his trademark of seeking a practical application to a specific problem.

That stance was equally mirrored in Anderson's approval of municipal reform – an early complementary fruit of parliamentary change – and its local effects. While 'a more upright and intelligent set of men had never held office than had been now called to it by their fellow citizens', he 'did not say this at the expense of their predecessors, because if he did so he should not only be doing injustice to their merits, but to his own feelings.' Such a detached and potentially controversial assessment in the charged atmosphere of reform was more than a judicious balancing act between Anderson's marital connections and his new political allies. It reflected a prevailing view that the Perth council in the decade prior to municipal reform had, as the new reformer lord provost himself stated, done 'the best they could under the rotten tree of corruption' and had even been distinguished for careful economy.

The limits of Anderson's appetite for political activism, and indeed of his liberalism, were delineated most clearly by the causes he failed to support, rather than those he did. Following the Reform Act he did not *publicly* champion, for instance, such Radical crusades as Corn Law repeal (despite occasional free trade utterances in his early correspondence), and the ballot or suffrage extension. In particular, further constitutional change was not on his personal agenda; the legislation of 1832-33 was a coping-stone. After its passage, apart from electoral support for Oliphant, Anderson openly endorsed only one liberal cause and it was foreign. In December 1833 an association was formed in Perth amid great enthusiasm to aid Polish refugees. A month later Men Zaba, accredited Scottish representative of Polish émigrés in Switzerland, was introduced by Anderson at a public meeting, as advocate 'of a brave and suffering people, whose only crime was that of having endeavoured to rescue their country from foreign thraldom and oppression.' In practice, Anderson's initiative was hardly controversial: sympathy for the victims of czarist autocracy encompassed virtually the entire domestic political spectrum.

When Oliphant was returned unopposed in the 1835 general election, Anderson was again one of his proposers. Characteristically, however, he denounced proposals through the hustings to subject the M.P. to pledges. Oliphant's parliamentary conduct, he contended, made them unnecessary. He actually found them repugnant *per se*, as a threat to an individual Member's independence. In 1837, Oliphant decided not to seek re-election, ostensibly for health reasons, but mainly due to polarisation of support to the reviving Tories and Whigs. His decision was communicated to the constituency through Anderson and others; with his departure, the latter virtually retired from active local politics. Exceptionally, and perhaps for personal rather than political reasons, he helped to secure the freedom of the Guildry in 1835 for Fox Maule, Whig Member for Perth county. Two years later, whatever his inclination, Anderson's migration to St Andrews precluded sustained active involvement in local politics. Nonetheless, after Maule switched to safer pastures as M.P. for Perth city, Anderson was induced in 1841, to appear at a Whig dinner and propose toasts to Maule's wife and Lord Lynedoch. In turn, he was acclaimed as 'a staunch and consistent Reformer whose time and money had been always ready to promote Liberal principles.'[30]

Despite this reputation, Anderson's relationships with Tory county gentry remained personally friendly. In 1835, for instance, he acted as steward at a public dinner welcoming the arrival of a male heir to Viscount Stormont, most prominent of local Tory aristocrats. This seemingly innocuous event generated a minor storm in the local political teacup. Several guests were vilified by partisan Whigs for associating with someone who, in Lord Provost Pringle's words, always 'arranged himself against the interests of the people'. Anderson's relative political detachment was recognised in his exclusion from the list of pilloried 'renegades'. It also found expression four years later in giving one of them, Baillie John Graham, a testimonial, when he applied for the governorship of the new general penitentiary in Perth. The virulence of the assault on Whigs, like Oliphant, who dared to socialise with the Tory foe, signalled the end of the non-party alliance personified by Anderson. The formation of the city's first official Conservative association in 1834, was another straw in the wind. Oliphant's withdrawal in 1837, following the disintegration of his electoral coalition, left the field to Tories and Whigs: predictably, Anderson abstained.[31] The Tory, Esdaile, subsequently asserted that, while he and Anderson were supposed to differ in politics, they had 'never been able to discover distinctly in what the difference consists'. This glossed over reality. As late as 1837, the reverend gentleman still regretted the Reform Act, anticipating little good to come from it and fearful of disappointed expectations.[32] By contrast, Anderson firmly endorsed that 'healing measure' and this was to constitute a major personal handicap in 1837, when attempting to secure a chair at St Andrews University.

But that was still a future problem. In the early 1830s Anderson was engrossed with a more immediate mission, which once again had political overtones and was rooted in his innate conservatism. He chose to make a personal contribution to social and political stability outwith the parameters of conventional politics - by promoting working-class education. The cause had great appeal: it promised moral elevation, a practical application of the Calvinist social conscience, public reconciliation of science and religion, and the deflection of working-class energies from more dangerous outlets. In short, it encompassed his personal priorities.

In the early nineteenth century the quality of education open to different social levels depended substantially on individual capacity to pay. Perth Academy was the apex of a relatively extensive provision of opportunity by the local council but, though complemented by private venture schools, the system was primarily targeted at middle-class consumption. The inadequacy of charity school provision for the needs of a new urban proletariat was clearly evinced in a survey by the council's own education committee in 1834. Undertaken appropriately in the year the Reverend George Lewis published his disturbingly-entitled polemic, *Scotland, a half-educated nation*, the council's survey revealed that 41% of Perth children between the ages of five and fourteen attended no school and that in working-class ghettoes, south-west of the town centre, abstention was almost universal. As an elder, Anderson probably collected data for this investigation, a task entrusted to kirk sessions. He was acutely aware of the educational desert being recorded in the Pomarium area, bounding his sessional district and within the parish, but his concern anticipated the survey. Although the academy was aimed mainly at the fee-paying middle-classes, he had previously pointed out that it was not exclusively a preserve of the rich: each year it educated a number of poor children gratis.[33]

As the town's most eminent salaried teacher he had regularly examined institutions recruiting children from humble backgrounds. These included Stewart's Free School, founded in 1813, with support from the Trades, and Graham's school for the poor, erected about 1820 and largely dependent on Lord Gray's patronage. In the latter, approximately four hundred children were taught to read the Bible and given elementary religious education. Such schools had clear limitations and the 1834 survey reiterated that the totality of provision, given the scale of need, made little impact. Accordingly, in 1835, a public meeting resolved to raise a subscription and apply for a Treasury grant to set up four new schools in destitute parts of the city. Anderson was elected to the fund-raising committee that collaborated with the council in pursuit of the objective. Unhappily, negotiations with the Treasury came unstuck, but not at least before two 'national' schools for poor children were founded at Newrow and Watergate.[34]

Anderson's commitment to working-class education was revealed most clearly, however, in his single-minded promotion of a mechanics' institute. The antecedent of this venture was modest: a mechanics' reading society started in 1823, with the limited aim of providing a library for working men. Despite sporadic advocacy in the local press in 1825, it was three years before a significant movement of public opinion, supported by several 'scientific gentlemen', gave credence to the concept of a fully-fledged institute. Anderson was undoubtedly a prime mover, but it took another two years to reach maturity. In October 1830, at a public meeting convened by a steering committee, he read an address, subsequently printed and circulated, on principles underlying mechanics' institutes. Such bodies were not visionary or untried, Anderson asserted, but had already produced 'the happiest effects upon that class of society for whose benefit' they were intended. Optimistically, and with academic bias, he opined that 'serene satisfaction' sprang from acquiring scientific knowledge, but it also had to be 'useful and salutary'. Such a syllabus apparently embraced arithmetic, mathematics, 'as much geometry as is necessary for the delineation of plans, machinery, etc.', dynamics, physics, mechanics, hydrostatics and pneumatics. The keystone of all sciences in this ambitious programme again mirrored his personal predilection at the academy for chemistry, which he deemed — in this context less obviously — the most useful subject for artisans. Yet the proposed curriculum was not exclusively scientific: natural theology and a desire to nip atheistic tendencies in the bud also featured in his thinking. So moral philosophy and Christian ethics should be included, 'to prevent the mind from being led astray by the vain and foolish delusions, to which those, whose attention is exclusively devoted to the pursuits of physical science, seem peculiarly liable.'

Besides concern for the dissemination of scientific knowledge and for working-class education as good in their own right, Anderson's dedication is explicable mainly within the framework of his general political outlook, in particular of the progressive conservatism manifested elsewhere in support for moderate parliamentary reform. He refuted 'the detestable, and the now happily-exploded maxim' that communicating knowledge to the labouring classes was dangerous; such notions stemmed from 'those who are interested in supporting abuses and perpetuating the existence of error'. The masses, he contended:

> [Could no longer] remain destitute of the advantages which the light of science has begun to shed over the face of civil society - and the best security that can be obtained for the preservation of our invaluable constitution, and the correction of the abuses which tarnish its excellencies, is to be found in the diffusion of sound knowledge and the encouragement of the arts of peaceful industry.

This optimistic view, that working-class intellects could be diverted from radicalism to 'useful knowledge', inevitably begged questions as to whether 'knowledge' really meant sedation and to whom it would be 'useful'. With growing working-class interest in further political reform, however, the middle-classes clutched at his straw. Several joined the interim committee and Anderson was eulogised as someone eminently qualified to initiate and superintend the venture.

Within five weeks of inauguration three hundred students were enrolled, a number greatly exceeding expectations, and plans were soon afoot to deploy anticipated donations to purchase books and equipment. The local press was ecstatic, detecting in the guiding hand a social reformist mission that would rescue young men from 'idleness and the worst habits'. Anderson's initial offer of gratuitous weekly lectures on arithmetic and geometry eased potential financial burdens and, in response to demand, he also readily agreed to include chemistry. By early November, subscriptions and donations flowed in steadily and Sir Alexander Muir Mackenzie became the institute's patron. An annual membership fee of 6/-, payable in monthly instalments, ensured a reasonably wide social base among skilled artisans, but social mobility was not intended. 'Well-regulated knowledge' was merely envisaged by the body's conservative promoters to 'fit the mechanic in his sphere intelligently for the business of life'. An emphasis on religiosity, Anderson's other *leitmotiv*, also shone through his inaugural lecture. It was 'not only beautiful, truly philosophical, and scientific thought, but marked with striking views of the gospel ... leading the contemplations of the students up to nature's God and the Redeemer.' Subsequently, Anderson twinned political conservatism and natural theology again, explaining that his object was to inculcate in members their duty to each other, to their Creator, and make them 'good members of society in this world'. Even more ambitiously, in an echo of his discarded clerical vocation, he sought to equip them for the next — 'for entering upon that immortal state of being where their faculties and knowledge would continue to be expanded.'[35]

Though considerably assisted by his academy colleague, Thomas Bruce, the teaching burden on Anderson increased, especially after an additional evening was gratuitously devoted to algebra. This reflected the widespread problem of institutes in maintaining continuity of adequate financial support from middle-class sympathisers after the initial impetus had dissipated. Thus in early 1831 plans for a scientific library were temporarily shelved, while Anderson's sole pecuniary recompense was a gift of spectacles set in gold, presented by appreciative students. Nonetheless, much appeared to have been accomplished by the second year: a library was initiated, nearly five hundred donors and subscribers attracted, and fulsome praise for their 'assiduity and abilities' heaped on many mechanics, to whom Anderson awarded prizes. He continued to direct the institute and lecturing duties were rationalised. Concentrating on physics and chemistry himself, he left Bruce to teach mathematics. Anderson maintained audience attention by supplementing his natural gift of popular presentation with the deliberate inclusion of a wide variety of experiments. Controversially, for twenty-first century sensitivities, some of these were admittedly horrendous in their use of live animals, a strange contradiction in a confirmed dog lover, who condemned blood sports in Germany and Spain as 'revolting'.[36]

Despite success in attracting individual donations from county gentry however, inadequate funding and declining support were endemic. By 1833, attendance had fallen to two hundred. A total income of merely £116.18s from all sources had to meet all expenditure, such as room rent, apparatus, and lecturing fees; the rector's own lectures continued to be given gratuitously, which helped to balance accounts. George Lewis cited Anderson's Perth initiative in his 1834 Glasgow Educational Association pamphlet on the prevailing state of Scotland's education. In an appendix to the tract, it was part of the evidence for the author's contention that - 'on the whole' - mechanics' institutions throughout Scotland were declining and afflicted by chronic under-funding.[37] Anderson's difficulties were not unique, and expedients, such as free admission to the introductory lecture for prospective students in 1834, underlined the waning of first enthusiasm. The council helped by providing accommodation in the academy and a free gas supply, but then split over the issue of giving further financial assistance. Some feared that municipal patronage would extinguish the voluntary impulse, sacred to contemporary middle-class minds; eventually £10 was offered to appoint a salaried lecturer. Anderson and Bruce were understandably weary of carrying the entire teaching load on a purely voluntary basis, but the request for help itself betrayed crumbling momentum. In response to the council's offer, the institute secretary could only hope that excellent premises would put 'new life' into the association.

Whether lectures continued beyond the 1834 session is uncertain. Two years later, Anderson at least was unavailable, following his move to St Andrews. Activities had been suspended sometime, however, when his successor as rector, Thomas Miller, revived the institute in January 1839. Although the curriculum remained the same, it no longer aimed exclusively at operatives, but set out to attract young middle-class professionals.[38] If Anderson's achievement seemed short-lived, he ran aground on a recurring reef. All subsequent attempts to provide adult education part-time for working-class consumption also attained limited success with their prime objective, but evoked and partly satisfied a largely unsought appetite for education among the middle-classes. The aim of diverting working-class energies from radicalism was, of course, doomed from the start. If anything, widening horizons fuelled aspirations to share political power.

NOTES

[1] *Science and religion in the nineteenth century;* ed. by Tess Cosslett, (Cambridge: Cambridge U.P., 1984), 25-7.

[2] C. Cowan, *Reminiscences*, (privately printed, 1878), 169.

[3] Univ. St And. Libr., Spec. Coll., TCL, Ms 30385/1. A. Anderson to T. Chalmers, Perth, 19 Nov. 1818.

[4] NCL, TCP, CHA. 4.258.23. Same to same, Perth, [1837]

[5] *Greenock Advertiser*, 2 and 9 Oct. 1840; *Fife Herald*, 10 Dec. 1846; H. Cockburn, *Journal of Henry Cockburn... 1831-1854*, (Edinburgh: Edmonston and Douglas, 1874), vol. 1, 117n. For an account of the controversial background to the joint Chalmers-Anderson lecture tour in Greenock, see W. Hanna, *Memoirs of the Life and Writings of Thomas Chalmers*, D.D., LL.D., (Edinburgh: Constable, 1852), vol. iv, 207-10.

[6] [Edinburgh:] N[ational] A[rchives of] S[cotland, HM General Register House], CH2/585/1, P[erth] E[ast] K[irk | S[ession] Min[utes], 8 Dec. 1811, 29 Mar. 1818.

[7] Adam Anderson, *Hints on the duty of contributing to the dissemination of the Scriptures, delivered at the last annual meeting of the Perthshire Bible Society*, ([Perth]: 1821).

[8] NCL, TCP, CHA. 4.65.29. A. Anderson to T. Chalmers, Perth, 29 May 1827.

[9] *Perth Courier*, 3 and 24 July 1834, 30 Mar. 1837; *Report of the speeches delivered at a dinner given to the Reverend James Esdaile... by some of the admirers of his defence of church establishments*, (Perth: 1834), 3, 65, 69-71.

[10] NAS, PGKS Min., 3 Mar., 20 Apr. 1836; *Perth Courier*, 8 Sep. 1842.

[11] NCL, TCP, CHA. 4.65.33. A. Anderson to T. Chalmers, Perth, 3 Nov. 1827.

12 NCL, TCP, CHA. 4.88.20. Same to same, Perth, 14 Feb. 1828; TCP, CHA. 4.245.13. Same to same, Perth, 15 Oct. 1836.

13 Univ. St And. Libr., Spec. Coll., MS38329/42. A. Anderson to parents, Edinburgh, 9 July 1806.

14 Univ. St And. Libr., Spec. Coll., MS38329/36. A. Anderson to parents, Edinburgh, 16 June 1805.

15 A. Jervise, *The history and traditions of the lands of the Lindsays*, 2nd ed., (Edinburgh: D. Douglas, 1882), 237-8, 276-8; NLS, Lee papers, Ms 3441/f375. J. Esdaile to Principal Lee, Perth, 5 June 1837.

16 Univ. St And. Libr., Spec. Coll., MS38329/52. A. Anderson to parents, Perth, 7 November 1809.

17 *OPR* 387/23, Parish of Perth, register of marriages. Carved artifacts, including a heart-shaped wooden box, a sketch, and surviving poems addressed to Agnes, written in a contemporary, sentimental style, all in furtherance of Anderson's suit, 1813-15, are still in family possession.

18 [Edinburgh:] N[ational] A[rchives of] S[cotland], Melville Castle papers, GD 51/6/2059(5). James Ramsay to the Duke of Athole, Perth, 23 Dec. 1819; T.C. Smout, *A history of the Scottish people, 1560-1830*, 2nd ed., (London: Collins, 1970), 444.

19 *Perth Courier*, 15 Dec. 1825, 4 May 1826; [Edinburgh:] N[ational] A[rchives of] S[cotland], Register of Sasines, RS/170/232, Perth, 26 May 1830; Perth Academy. xerox copies of correspondence from Adam Anderson to Andrew Anderson, jun., [son], Croft [Perth], 1844-46. Anderson acquired lots 8 and 9 in St Leonard's Bank on 26 May 1830. Feu conditions required him to construct a house of not less than £800 value, with a front of ashlar or hammer dressed course work and a roof of the best dark blue slates.

20 *Perth Courier*, 2 Aug. 1822, 23 May 1823, 20 Nov. 1828, 24 Sep. 1829, 18 Nov. 1830, 5 May 1831, 17 Nov. 1836; T.D. Miller, *The History of the Royal Perth Golfing Society*, (Perth: Munro Press, 1935), 16.

21 *Perth Courier*, 7 Feb. 1811, 1 and 8 Feb. 1816, 8 May 1817, 21 Sep. 1826, 16 Oct. 1828, 6 Jan. 1831, 8 Mar. 1832.

22 *ibid.*, 22 and 29 Mar., 12 Apr. 1832, 4 Dec. 1834, 6 Oct. 1836.

23 NCL, TCP, CHA. 4.172.27. A. Anderson to T. Chalmers, Perth, 30 Apr. 1832.

24 *Perth Courier*, 5 Oct. 1820.

25 NLS, Lee papers, Ms 3441/f375. J. Esdaile to Principal Lee, Perth, 5 June 1837.

26 NAS, Melville Castle papers, GD 51/6/2059(4). Lord Gray to the Duke of Athole, Kinfauns Castle, 24 Dec. 1819.

27 *Perth Courier*, 28 Apr., 5 and 12 May 1831; NLS, Lee papers, Ms 3441/f375. J. Esdaile to Principal Lee, Perth, 5 June 1837.

28 *Perth Courier*, 28 Apr. 1831; PTC Corr., bundle 432. Sir Alexander Muir Mackenzie to Lord Provost P.G. Stewart, Delvine, 3 June 1831.

29 Sir Thomas Dick Lauder, *Memorial of the royal progress in Scotland*, (Edinburgh: Black, 1843), 238-9; *Perth Courier*, 3 and 17 May, 9 Aug. 1832.

30 *ibid.*, 5 July, 2 and 9 Aug., 4 Oct., 22 and 29 Nov., 6, 13, 20 and 27 Dec. 1832, 28 Nov., 5 Dec. 1833, 16 Jan. 1834, 15 and 22 Jan. 1835, 15 June 1837; *Perthshire Advertiser*, 22 July 1841.

31 *Perth Courier*, 13 and 20 Aug. 1835, 3 Oct. 1839; Perth: A K Bell Library. *List of the constituency of the city of Perth*, 1837, 11.

32 NLS, Lee papers, Ms 3441/f375. J. Esdaile to Principal Lee, Perth, 5 June 1837.

33 A.W. Harding, *op. cit.*, vol. 2, 499-537; PEKS Min., 7 Dec. 1834; *Perth Courier*, 28 Nov. 1833.

34 *ibid.*, 22 July 1819, 14 June 1822, 26 Feb., 5 Mar. 1835; A.W. Harding, *op.cit.*, vol. 2, 525-8, 535-7.

35 *ibid.*, vol. 2, 540; *Perth Courier*, 20 May, 3 and 23 June 1825, 23 Feb. 1826, 29 May, 25 Dec. 1828, 30 Sep., 21 and 28 Oct., 4 Nov., 2 and 16 Dec. 1830.

36 Perth Academy. [xerox copy]. A. Anderson to Andrew Anderson, jun., [son], Croft [Perth], 15 Sep. 1845.

[37] G. Lewis: *Scotland: a half-educated nation, both in the quantity and quality of her educational institutions* (Glasgow: William Collins, [1834]), 94-95 (appendix on 'State of the Mechanics' Institutions of Scotland).

[38] *Perth Courier*, 2 Dec. 1830, 20 Jan., 21 July, 6 Oct., 3 Nov. 1831, 19 Apr., 14 June 1832, 9 and 30 Jan. 1834, 17 Jan., 14 Mar. 1839; PTC Min., 16 Jan., 3 Feb. 1834.

6

UNITED COLLEGE DISUNITED: SIR DAVID BREWSTER AND ST ANDREWS

Adam Anderson's political beliefs, or rather what they were represented to be, acquired crucial significance for his career in 1837, when he sought a chair at St Andrews University. This was not, of course, his first attempt to obtain an academic appointment there. As a divinity student in 1802, he had tried to become Vilant's part-time mathematics assistant. Four or five years later, as a family tutor, the prospect of a chair in either mathematics or chemistry also attracted his interest. By 1819, after ten years at Perth Academy, Anderson was ready for a new attempt to wrest the elusive mathematics chair. When the sitting incumbent, Dr Robert Haldane, the celebrated divine, emerged as probable inheritor of the principalship of St Mary's College, Anderson canvassed vigorously to replace him in the chair. In May of that year his friend, Lord Gray of Kinfauns, enthusiastically extolled Anderson's claims in respect of character and scientific attainment to the university chancellor, Viscount Melville, contending that there was 'not a man in Scotland better fitted for a Professor's chair'.[1] When Haldane's possible elevation surfaced a few months later, Gray was once more active. Approached by Anderson's father-in-law, ex-Lord Provost Ramsay,[2] Gray in turn lobbied the Duke of Athole, assuring him of the candidate's mathematical abilities and, more pertinently, of his political reliability in the government interest. He persuaded Athole to intercede with Melville,[3] despite the Duke's lack of acquaintance with Anderson personally.[4] Even this extended chain of Conservative influence nonetheless, proved inadequate to realise Anderson's ambitions on that occasion. Strangely, he would be more successful eighteen years later, though by then in his mid-fifties and carrying a significant albatross around his neck - active participation in reform politics in the intervening period.

In early 1837 Anderson informed Chalmers of his intention to seek the natural philosophy chair at St Andrews, which had fallen vacant with the death of Thomas Jackson. To this old acquaintance, whose testimonial he required, an elaboration of his scientific pursuits or writings would be superfluous. He did remind him, however, of the practical application he had made 'of more than one department of science to the business of life', citing specifically the request through Sir F. French, M.P. for Scarborough, of a sketch and description of the Perth water works for transmission to the King of Prussia.[5] Anderson also attempted to enlist support from the brilliant young holder of the natural philosophy chair at Edinburgh, James D. Forbes, who had unexpectedly called on him to introduce himself the previous summer.[6] Although Forbes was slightly embarrassed by this approach, since Edinburgh candidates were also in the field and he did not wish to judge respective merits, his response was encouraging. He promised, 'if applied to', freely and unhesitatingly to express his high opinion of Anderson's services to meteorology in general and to hygrometry in particular. His visit to Perth had not been fruitless; he had borrowed and imitated the rector's 'excellent illustration of Parabolic motion'. More important, Anderson was permitted to use his reply effectively as a testimonial, 'if this merely friendly letter could be of any service ... without seeming partial.'[7]

The approach to Forbes was timely: only six days later the Edinburgh physicist was contacted by Thomas Duncan, Whig professor of mathematics at St Andrews, with a request for an assessment of Anderson, whose articles he assumed would be familiar.[8] The precise nature of Duncan's questions apparently relieved Forbes of scruples in answering them. He acknowledged an early familiarity with Anderson's writings on meteorology and indeed had already cited them in two British Association reports. Nonetheless, Forbes refreshed his memory by checking Brewster's *Encyclopaedia*. He admitted being impressed:

Not only as to the extensive acquaintance of Dr A. with the subject of which he treated but as to his genius for original enquiry which it is much to be regretted that circumstances (I suppose connected with his situation in Perth) have prevented him from carrying out. The variety of the subject matter contained in his Encyclopaedic contributions show acquaintance with a considerable range of the mixed sciences.

For good measure he speculated that his teaching role at Perth Academy 'would offer still further grounds of recommendation'.[9]

The support of eminent clerics, especially Evangelicals, and of scientific peers, was inadequate, of course, to obtain a chair in the conservative University of St Andrews in the 1830s: political as well as academic considerations were important. So in mid-April the new principal-designate of United College, John Lee, received Anderson's request for support and an assurance that Sir David Brewster would be writing on his behalf.[10] When it became clear, however, that the Tory professors resented Anderson's involvement in political Liberalism, pressure on Lee from more influential quarters to espouse his cause suddenly intensified. John A. Murray, Whig lord advocate, insisted that his attendance and support for Anderson, 'to which he is so well entitled from his own merits', were expected as a *quid pro quo* for Lee's own appointment. Murray trusted that Lee 'would not give occasion to the observations which your absence from this election might give rise to'.[11] The irrepressible Esdaile meantime assured Lee of Anderson's underlying conservatism and predicted that he would be 'an ornament to science and to society' in St Andrews.[12] Lee, not yet formally inducted as principal, saw that what was normally a virtual sinecure had a price. As his pleas of ill health clearly fell on deaf ears he eventually agreed to travel to St Andrews for the election. To remove any suspicion that he merely responded to political pressure however, he conveniently recalled that his impressions had been favourable from the start and were merely confirmed by commendation from others.[13] Brewster's support in particular had been critical, but he would have preferred not to have known 'whether Dr Anderson had any political support or no — I espouse his cause firstly as being a man of science and as having given proof of his sufficient aptitude for the office at which he aims.'[14]

Lee's arrival in St Andrews permitted his formal elevation as principal. The following day, 13 June, he presided over the election to the natural philosophy chair, giving his casting vote to Anderson over Dr Memes of Ayr Academy.[15] Informed of the result immediately by Lee, Anderson acknowledged that his support had been crucial, but tactfully suggested that the principal had been motivated only by considerations of relative merit. Lee's 'hints' about the electorate had also been noted, but with perhaps an eye to future working relations Anderson magnanimously suggested that his opponents acted from a conscientious concern for college interests.[16] On 3 August 1837, Anderson was formally inducted, while Lee prematurely resigned his principalship before the end of the year.[17] Ongoing controversy over his part in Anderson's elevation was a major element in his departure. The following February Anderson sympathised with Lee over continuing accusations of political jobbery from the Memes camp. He had solicited support personally on grounds of merit alone, had won in the teeth of deliberate distortion of his political opinions and, unlike his opponents, had been unwilling to seek pledges before all the candidates were known. It was ironical that someone with a reputation for avoiding controversy should gain his academic inheritance in such an embittered atmosphere: in Anderson's own words, he had seldom witnessed 'such a rare combination of indiscretion, arrogance, falsehood, and malignity'.[18] Unhappily his period at St Andrews was punctuated, through no fault of his own, with a succession of vitriolic disputes. These would focus, ironically, on Sir David Brewster, his old acquaintance and most influential academic referee, who succeeded Lee as principal of United College in March 1838.[19]

Meantime, the dispute over Anderson's appointment rapidly expired through his own impact on St Andrews. Although the town's population had climbed to nearly 3,800 by his return,[20] it remained a close-knit community dependent on good relations between town and gown for social harmony. Characteristically, Anderson flung himself into activities that captured local imagination, appealing particularly to prevailing lay interest in scientific enquiry. Soon after his arrival he set about recording observations of atmospheric phenomena of the east Fife coast with rain gauges installed on the college steeple and other sites.[21] Shortly afterwards, he provided public entertainment using solar rays and a concentrating mirror to produce an explosion and ignition in vials containing oxygen and other elements. The *Fife Herald* was delighted: science had been 'an Eleusinian mystery' at St Andrews for too long, it proclaimed, adding: 'Let her walk forth from her retreat and the public will meet her halfway.'[22]

The local Literary and Philosophical Society, in which Anderson was soon elected to office, was the principal forum for contact between university and local intellects. Anderson gave regular lectures and demonstrations on mathematics, astronomy, optics and other scientific disciplines until his death. In May 1845, he tested local enthusiasm for science by inviting members to join him at eight o'clock one morning to view a solar eclipse through his telescopes.[23] The adulation of the Whig *Herald*, which soon detected that 'a new soul' had 'been infused into our society by Dr Anderson's judicious accommodation to the spirits of the times',[24] was predictable, but the degree of his acceptance was reflected in the concurrent acclaim of the Tory *Fifeshire Journal*. By the beginning of 1838, it was willing to admit that the recent university appointments by the Whig government had been unexpectedly prudent:

> Though they have ... driven us to the inference that they have chosen their protégés, not because they were men of philosophy, but men of politics, they have chosen well - whiggery may thank *herself;*

and we may congratulate ourselves that reasons can be found why such men as Sir David Brewster and Dr Anderson should be appointed members of our university.

Brewster, it accepted, had gained 'golden opinions', and as for Anderson the belief was:

> That his only misfortune has been that amiable facility of temper which has often permitted him to be put in positions from which his good sense and cool judgement must have revolted. His bland and gentlemanly manners, his thorough knowledge of science, his extreme assiduity and perfect want of pretension, have not only overcome every prejudice in regard to the circumstances of his appointment, but occasioned the liveliest sensations lest his domestic arrangements elsewhere should by any chance deprive us, for some part of the year, of his presence.[25]

This last rumour proved to be true. Unable or unwilling to cut social ties with Perth, Anderson opted to camp with members of his family and domestic help in St Andrews during the relatively short academic sessions, returning to the former during vacations. In the last years of life he let his St Leonard's Bank house and during the vacations moved with his remaining family into the Ramsay household at the Croft. There, in 1846, he occupied a garret room which served as his 'workshop, library, w.c., and is as variously furnished as Noah's Ark'. Despite or due to these shortcomings, it answered his needs 'most admirably'.[26] A public role in Perth, if necessarily restricted, also continued. He still held office in the Literary and Antiquarian Society, subjected another generation of

Academy pupils to a more searching examination than witnesses could ever recall and, when dredging operations in the Tay led to a fall in the water level in the water works tank, returned to overcome the problem.[27]

Most time was devoted to academic science however, punctuated with the distraction of domestic worries. Professorial emoluments averaging £315 annually in 1837-40, probably exceeded his overall remuneration at the academy, and were supplemented by a significant rent from letting his house. Financial security allowed him greater mobility than before, while his new academic role provided more incentive to travel. Through the British Association for the Advancement of Science, a forum for the provincial scientific profession that found little in common with the metropolitan orientation of the Royal Society, he came into contact with others of a similar background. In June 1845, he attended the association's Cambridge meeting, when he exhibited patterns of reflected light from revolving mirrors on a ceiling and discussed their mathematical implications.[28]

Unhappily commitments appeared to extend with income and the immediate family was the prime cause. His daughter, Eliza, had married an Irish landlord whose rent income was disrupted firstly by O'Connellite sympathisers and then by the famine of the mid-1840s. An otherwise enjoyable visit to Cork in 1844, when Anderson was entertained with Irish gentry aboard a naval frigate, was spoilt when he was obliged, not for the last time, to give his son-in-law a subvention. Andrew, discontented with his chosen army career, especially after a posting in the unhealthy West Indies, also made recurrent demands.[29] Only two months before his own death, Anderson seized the opportunity of a visit to Perth by Fox Maule, newly-appointed Secretary-at-War, to lobby on his son's behalf. The promise of a post of paymaster with its guarantee of increased remuneration for gratifyingly little work appears to have been the result. Despite this, neither Andrew nor his sisters matched Anderson's admittedly exacting expectations of regular correspondents. A further more serious cloud, again with financial overtones, was the knowledge that the Ramsays' lease of the Croft was due to expire in 1847, and that responsibility for resettling his elderly, widowed mother-in-law and the combined household would fall on himself.[30] Above all, however, the end of his life was devastated by the serious illness of his vivacious daughter, Amelia Agnes. This prevented her accompanying him on his return to St Andrews in autumn 1844, and attendance at her deathbed in January delayed Anderson's departure to United College following the Christmas break. Months later he was still overwhelmed with grief, seeking solace in work, as he caught up on a backlog of deferred lectures to his students.[31]

As at Perth Academy Anderson's first task following his induction to St Andrews was to acquire adequate scientific apparatus. Even before his actual arrival to assume his appointment, he initiated the first of several requests for equipment. On occasion the tried tactic of making personal advances was deployed and by 1843, the college felt obliged to provide a new press for his expanding collection.[32] This accumulation reflected a preoccupation with public experiment to demonstrate scientific principles. The approach of his predecessor had been quite different. On Jackson's own admission, his equipment had been merely 'tolerably good' for his own class and would have been useless for a popular class. As he explained to the university commissioners, he did 'not exhibit a great variety of showy experiments, but rather such as are fundamental and scientific', preferring 'accuracy ... to show and mere amusement'.[33] Brewster shared the same condescending attitude. He had earlier argued that there was 'no profession so incompatible with original inquiry as a Scotch Professorship, where one's income depends on the number of pupils.' In his view the economic imperative to attract students and their fees converted them all into 'showmen', though such reservations did not deter him from an unsuccessful bid for the natural philosophy chair at Edinburgh two years later.[34]

Anderson endorsed Brewster's concern for original research, but believed that neither it nor accuracy was sacrificed by illumination. Rather he saw positive good in popularising science and identifying its practical applications. Though following in general the course offered by Jackson, his teaching was:

More amply illustrated in every department of the subject by experiment, as well as rendered more subservient to a knowledge of the various mechanical arts which administer to the comforts and enjoyments of civilized life, without any sacrifice of the great design at which we ought to aim in every course of scientific instruction, namely, the improvement of the moral and intellectual faculties of the student, by inuring his mind to habits of accurate research through severe and rigid investigation.[35]

Like his scholars in Perth, undergraduates in St Andrews warmed to this approach. At the close of the 1842-43 session, they presented a written testimonial commending his zeal and energy and noting the comprehensive composition of his teaching in the physical sciences. In particular they applauded the extra hours he set aside on Saturdays, 'in inculcating the popular branches of Natural Philosophy, and in exhibiting to us such a variety of experiments.'[36]

Despite an ingrained business-like approach, pecuniary self-interest was not his motive. While receiving a smaller income than most colleagues, Anderson regularly gave abatements of fees from two to three guineas to needy students and openly advocated a reduction for all alumni throughout the Scottish universities. Encouragement to unpopular but useful branches of science should be derived, he argued, not from fees but public endowment. If he spent only the actual academic sessions in Mrs Ireland's lodgings at St Andrews, Anderson's dedication as a university teacher was beyond reproach. Loneliness did not trouble him in exile, he confided to his son, due to activity preparing apparatus for lectures and examining student exercises in the evenings. His mode of discipline was the same as in Perth, conciliatory rather than coercive, but administered with firmness he found it to be equally effective with students, 'even upon stubborn and refractory dispositions.' At the same time he insisted on regularity of attendance, while rewarding diligence with prizes at the close of each session.[37]

Insofar as divided residence allowed, Anderson undertook a normal active role in university administration and politics. Because of his enumerative and engineering skills, he was frequently encumbered with auditing the college accounts, reviewing bursaries, and serving as master of works on the maintenance of college properties. His varied briefs ranged from the chapel roof to potential improvements to a farm steading owned by the college at Scooniehill.[38] More important than these chores was the pressing question of rebuilding the university, the dominant issue since the 1826 Royal Commission visitation. With some judicious exaggeration by both professors and commissioners, the indisputably dilapidated state of the colleges had been carefully documented. The natural philosophy classroom, by no means the worst, featured in the inventory of complaint: inadequate in size for the disposition of even Jackson's modest equipment, it was penetrated by smoke from the vicinity of the steeple to such an extent that in the morning the shape of the window could not be discerned until thrown open to let the smoke escape. Jackson's principal grievance however, apart from the size of rooms, related to the overall impression: without a new building the college accommodation would be such that they would be 'ashamed to show it to any stranger, especially to any Englishman'.[39]

Following the visitation, pressure from Lord Melville and the commissioners secured Treasury grants which repaired St Mary's, but an elegant plan by Robert Reid, King's Architect for Scotland, foundered. An east wing for United College quadrangle was completed in 1831, but it provided few additional classrooms and these at a cost that prejudiced construction of a proposed north wing. With the transfer of outstanding Treasury aid to Aberdeen's Marischal College as a result of the delay, an impasse ensued which remained unresolved when Anderson arrived.[40] During his first month on the college council, however, the problem resurfaced when it was decided to petition the lord advocate for his intervention. Concurrently the council reaffirmed that the completion of the buildings was 'essential to the respectability and cumfort [sic] of this ancient seminary'. Unhappily, due to a House of Commons regulation, the lord advocate felt obliged through Brewster to decline the request. The council was unimpressed and, believing that the technicality could be overcome, asked Anderson in February 1838, to contact the principal-designate and seek his view on how it should respond. At the end of the year Brewster and Anderson were still jointly embroiled with the issue; they lobbied the under-secretary of state, Fox Maule, during a visit to Scotland, and were requested by him to prepare a memorial for Lord Melbourne's attention. But this frenetic activity among Anderson's political connections failed to prise open the Treasury's grasp. Not until Major Hugh Playfair, energetic provost of St Andrews, was appointed college agent five years later to secure a public grant, did events take shape. Largely through his influence a modified plan for the north wing was executed in 1845-46.[41] Anderson acknowledged that Playfair was also primarily responsible for the concurrent rebuilding of St Andrews — 'so much altered ... you would scarcely recognise it to be the same town' — and in 1844 helped to sponsor a public dinner in his honour.[42]

A more innovative contribution to the university by Anderson was made in terms of curricular evolution. A year after his arrival he served with Brewster and Briggs on a committee to consider the potential role of civil engineering. Its remit was subsequently extended to assess whether future changes should be made in duties discharged by several professors.[43] Ten months later the committee proposed wide-ranging reforms to the entire curriculum. These included making civil history compulsory; placing logic, rhetoric and metaphysics on an equal footing with moral philosophy; advertising Dr Cook's lectures on political economy; reviving natural history; and advertising as a course, in connection with natural philosophy, the civil engineering lectures which Anderson had already introduced, while 'not interfering with the more scientific course which occupies his first hour.' Owing to the outright refusal of its influential professor to comply, the pre-eminence of moral philosophy over other philosophical disciplines remained, but the other recommendations were adopted. This was a step away from the traditional, clericalist and humanist curriculum of the university, towards one that was more modern and balanced, and with an augmented role for science. Just how modern this curricular development was may be gauged by placing civil engineering as an academic discipline in historic perspective. Although engineering was taught at Cambridge as early as 1776, nearly a century elapsed before a chair was established there. One was incorporated in newly founded University College, London, in 1827, but remained effectively unfilled until 1841. Rival King's College and, briefly, Durham manifested early interest, while Glasgow engaged a practising civil engineer as first professor in 1840. Nonetheless, as late as 1870 only seven centres throughout Britain offered higher education in engineering.[44] If St Andrews seems in retrospect an improbable nurturing ground for such a venture, it was still a courageous attempt at radical reform when the locational disadvantages were less obvious than later.

Significantly, the package was advocated on its relevance to altered educational and societal needs in the outside world: 'the course of instruction could be rendered more proficient and better adapted to the changes which have taken place in professional education.' Consistent with this attitude was the stand taken in senate two years later by the modernising lobby - Brewster, Anderson and Duncan - over the vacant Chandos chair of medicine and anatomy. They opposed the appointment of Dr Reid, superintendent of Edinburgh Royal Infirmary, since it pre-empted the wishes of the royal commissioners that a vacancy in medicine or civil history should be converted into a chair of natural history or modern languages. A written undertaking had even been given to consult the commission and the majority decision put at risk 'these measures for the benefit of the University and for the interests of the Professors which they might otherwise have done.' United College, they added, was decidedly of the opinion that botany, mineralogy, geology, meteorology and other indispensable branches of natural history were essential to the university curriculum, whereas medicine had been a sinecure as a chair for ninety years and as a subject even longer. Public expectations should not be disappointed, they argued, but this view of public accountability in the age of reform was not shared by traditionalists in senate who confirmed Reid's appointment by eight votes to three.[45]

The early identification of Anderson with Sir David Brewster at St Andrews was scarcely surprising. Besides a long-standing acquaintance and Brewster's contribution to his appointment, their careers had several points of comparison. Whilst they shared interests in the physical sciences, both were devout Christians, had studied divinity at Edinburgh University, had experienced similar tensions between the claims of science and religion, and had eventually opted for the former. Brewster's passion for practical reform and the abolition of sinecures, a crusade launched by transforming his own principalship into a working appointment, also elicited Anderson's sympathy. If it was true that Brewster's allegations of financial mismanagement and corruption by the professoriate were provocatively specific charges in a small intimate society, Anderson's sentiments were expressed equally frankly. 'Much odium and reproach', he told the university commissioners in 1840, could not fail to be incurred by the 'mercenary' sale of academical degrees to eke out inadequate professorial stipends. He summed up bluntly: 'while less honour is conferred ... upon those who receive the degree, a positive disgrace is inflicted upon those who bestow it.'[46]

Unfortunately, identity of interest between Anderson and Brewster became one of several casualties of the impatience, irascibility, pugnacity and general lack of tact, which characterised the principal's sojourn at St Andrews. Although an apologist claimed in Brewster's mitigation, that he was at least not vindictive,[47] arguably he made an exception in Anderson's case. He was at loggerheads, of course, with all members of United College, but Anderson appears to have been singled out for particular attention. Whether this was due more to Brewster's reaction against previous friendship, rivalry within the same academic discipline, or sheer misfortune, is a moot point. One element in the rift, and indeed between the principal and the academic community generally in this stronghold of Moderatism, stemmed from the approaching schism in the Established Kirk. While Anderson was evangelical in outlook, Brewster was an Evangelical by affiliation. As late as 1840, the distinction was obscured. That February the principal persuaded all but two members of United College to grant the use of the college chapel for a non-intrusion meeting; Anderson was among the majority.[48] Three years later, on the eve of the Disruption, and ironically with their mutual friend, Chalmers, as the *cause célèbre*, Brewster was at odds with his colleagues, including Anderson. He and two other professors received letters from the principal asserting that he had 'authority over all persons and things' within the college. In particular he required them to admit to the humanity class Daniel Stewart, a student who had been 'illegally' expelled by their votes and those of other members of senate, 'pretending to exercise the power of the Rector and his assessors'. If still denied admission, Brewster intended to hold the trio personally responsible for an 'act of injustice' to a meritorious student, and of insubordination to authority under which, he contended, they were placed. Stewart and his fellow alumni had, in fact, been disciplined for electing Thomas Chalmers rector of the university on 6 March 1843. Since eligibility for the office was confined by tradition to only four senior figures within the university, the 'election' was strictly illegal, but fortified by Brewster's support, the students refused to be admonished. Facing this typically provocative challenge from Brewster, senate authorised Anderson and his colleagues to carry out the expulsions. It also reported the dispute fully to the chancellor, Lord Melville, in the hope of his intervention. In the event the commissioners reinstated the students, though the adjudication went against them, but Brewster was reprimanded for exceeding his powers.[49]

Shortly afterwards the Disruption widened the split in the university. In November United College, including Anderson, considered whether Brewster's adherence to the Evangelical protest at the General Assembly had signified his secession from the Establishment and thus legally disqualified him from the principalship and its emoluments. Though unwilling to preclude his attendance, they reserved recognition of his position pending judicial clarification. In subsequent proceedings against Brewster by the Established Presbytery of St Andrews, attempting to eject him from office following his adherence to the Free Kirk, the only member of the academic community to openly declare for him was Ferrie.[50] By then Anderson's alienation from Brewster, Chalmers and the Evangelical cause was summed up in uncharacteristically waspish comments to his son. These recounted an incident in which members of the principal's family had galloped through St Andrews – 'all greatly delighted with their own equestrian performances though scarcely in accord with the effected [sic] sanctity of members of the Free Kirk.'[51]

Brewster's temperament combined with the crisis in religious politics ensured a quarrel with virtually every academic at United College in the Disruption era, but in Anderson's case the scope for collision was enhanced by their original link: a common interest in the physical sciences. With Brewster a continuing scholar, not merely an administrator, the ingredients of conflict were present. The principal had neither his own apparatus nor lecture theatre, so resorting to the use of the natural philosophy classroom was unavoidable. Consequently, he and Anderson sometimes spent hours putting up and clearing away the latter's equipment, which Anderson had then to re-erect for his next lecture. Likewise, Brewster could only illustrate his own teaching by clearing the blackboards of Anderson's formulae and diagrams.[52] In November 1842, Brewster intimated, through the college porter, his intention of taking over the classroom on Saturdays. Instructions for the removal of Anderson's apparatus prior to the first meeting were also issued. Anxious at this point to be conciliatory, the council arranged to assign the principal the humanity classroom instead. Three days later, a further concession was made: if Anderson (who was not present) agreed, and provided that the use of his room was 'absolutely necessary for such experiments as require the exclusion of light', Brewster could use it 'for that particular purpose' upon adequate notice being given to the usual occupant to permit necessary arrangements to be made. The council preferred nevertheless, to put shutters on the humanity classroom windows, if these were considered essential.

Three months later, the principal precipitated renewed confrontation by commencing a series of weekly lectures on mineralogy in Anderson's room on Tuesday afternoons. Exasperated by the latest example of Brewster's quixotic streak, his partisanship, and his defiance of past practice by allowing students to transfer their allegiance from the college chapel to the church of the Reverend Ralph Robb, a hardline Evangelical, United College was now equally truculent. It authorised Anderson to retain possession of his room and recommended Brewster to fit up an old classroom or use the humanity room, 'always provided that Sir David guarantee that the seats be not in any degree injured.' Ignoring this, the principal entered the natural philosophy classroom again a week later, maintaining his right to teach in any room of the college. Anderson, preparing apparatus for a lecture, was forcibly thrust aside and, when his foot slipped, Brewster walked over him in triumph to the platform. The Tory *Fifeshire Journal* poked fun at the Evangelical principal's 'intrusion', but the college was less amused. An interdict was initiated in the Court of Session and served by the sheriff of Fife. This prohibited him from entering Anderson's or any other classroom for lecturing purposes without the consent of both council and the particular professor. After an abortive attempt to obtain the use of the local Secession kirk, Brewster announced his intention of defying the courts. On the appointed date he approached Anderson's room, flanked by supporters, but at the last moment accepted the offer of another classroom rather than risk 'the tender mercies of the Court of Session'. A subsequent request to have the interdict lifted upon sufficient guarantee of Brewster's non-interference with Anderson's room was rejected by council. Like so many other disputes between principal and college, it was referred to the royal commissioners. Having heard Brewster and Anderson plead their respective cases, they resolved that the former could use the accommodation on Saturdays, but left the issue of access during the week to the adjudication of Dr Buist, pro-rector, once he had heard both parties.[53]

A further confrontation with Brewster followed a fatal accident to the eleven-year-old son of Thomas Peattie, a porter at United College, in December 1845. While delivering coals to the natural philosophy classroom, curiosity induced the boy to open a gasometer stopcock, whilst carrying a lighted candle in his hand. The subsequent explosion killed him almost instantaneously. Brewster seized the opportunity to humiliate Anderson, circulating details of the tragedy to other prominent physicists, including Forbes, in the hope of eliciting condemnations. Claiming that he had received letters from professors Cumming of Cambridge and Andreas of Belfast castigating 'great carelessness in the party which left such a dangerous mixture in such a vessel for such a length of time', Brewster fired a series of leading questions at the Edinburgh physicist. He asked Forbes whether he conducted experiments requiring a mixture of oxygen and hydrogen in one vessel with a common stopcock; whether it was careless to leave such a mixture for nine or ten days in an apartment open to students, porters and others without advertising the danger; and whether experiments requiring such a mixture would not be better made by keeping the gases separate and mixing them prior to the lecture.[54] Forbes' reply is unknown, but Brewster followed up his correspondence with an attack on Anderson at a college meeting in January 1846, when the latter countered by demanding an enquiry.[55] Thereupon the matter appears to have been laid to rest.

In the context of contemporary health and safety thinking, events like the Peattie death were considered regrettable rather than avoidable, but the impact on Anderson was greater than appeared at first. Allegations of culpability, following the stress of repeated confrontations with the principal, undoubtedly took their toll on the health of an individual whose natural instinct was to shy clear of conflict. These trials moreover followed hard on the heels of the depression engendered by his daughter's death. Less than a year later, in the morning of 5 December 1846, a servant found Anderson dead in bed. No obvious sign of physical ill health had appeared until the preceding day when he consulted Dr Reid with suspected heart trouble. Despite this he took one of his timetabled classes before spending three hours in preparation for his Saturday popular lectures. Retiring to his lodgings much fatigued, breathless, and unable to eat, he was examined again by his physician. Early the following morning he died - a dose of medication untouched by his bedside. The cause of death was diagnosed as aneurysm. Reporting his passing to ex-Principal Lee, William Spalding, professor of logic, inadvertently placed his finger on the ultimate cause of death when he reflected:

Poor Anderson! He was only too gentle
and quiet for us! One of the best things he
did in College business was to put a stop to
a new attack of the scoundrel Brewster, by
declaring his willingness once more to give
the use of his rooms for the fellow's quack
lectures.[56]

NOTES

1. Univ. St And. Libr., Spec. Coll., Ms 4568. Lord Gray to Viscount Melville, Kinfauns Castle, 28 May 1819.

2. NAS, Melville Castle papers, GD 51/6/2059(5). James Ramsay to the Duke of Athole, Perth, 23 Dec. 1819.

3. NAS, Melville Castle papers, GD 51/6/2059(3-4). Lord Gray to same, Kinfauns Castle, 24 Dec. 1819; Duke of Athole to Viscount Melville, London, 30 Dec. 1819.

4. NAS, Melville Castle papers, GD 51/6/2059(1-2). A. Anderson to Sir P. Murray, Perth, 27 Dec. 1819; Sir P. Murray to Viscount Melville, Ochtertyre, 29 Dec. 1819.

5. NCL, TCP, CHA. 4.258.23. A. Anderson to T. Chalmers, Perth, [1837].

6. Univ. St And. Libr., Spec. Coll., [J.D.] Forbes papers, incoming letters, 1837/38, Ms deposit 7, Ms 14. Same to J.D. Forbes, Perth, 21 Mar. 1837.

7. Univ. St And. Libr., Spec. Coll., Forbes papers, letterbook 11, copy outgoing letterbook, 1837/437. J.D. Forbes to A. Anderson, Edinburgh, 23 Mar. 1837.

8. Univ. St And. Libr., Spec. Coll., Forbes papers, incoming letters, 1837/15. Thomas Duncan to J.D. Forbes, St Andrews, 27 Mar. 1837.

9. Univ. St And. Libr., Spec. Coll., Forbes papers, letterbook 11, copy outgoing letterbook, 1837/445. J.D. Forbes to Thomas Duncan, Edinburgh, 1 Apr. 1837.

10. NLS, Lee papers, Ms 3441/ff347-8. A. Anderson to Principal Lee, Perth, 13 Apr. 1837.

11 NLS, Lee papers, Ms 3441/ff369-72. John A. Murray to same, London, 1 June 1837.

12 NLS, Lee papers, Ms 3441/f375. J. Esdaile to same, Perth, 5 June 1837.

13 NLS, Lee papers, Ms 3441/f379. Principal Lee [to John A. Murray?], Edinburgh, 7 June 1837.

14 NLS, Lee papers, Ms 3441/ff380-81. Principal Lee to Fox Maule, Edinburgh, 7 June 1837.

15 Univ. St And. Libr., Spec. Coll., UC 400, U[nited] C[ollege] Min[utes], 12 and 13 June 1837; *Fifeshire Journal*, 15 June 1837.

16 NLS, Lee papers, Ms 3441/f384. A. Anderson to Principal Lee, Perth, 14 June 1837.

17 Univ. St And. Libr., Spec. Coll., UC 400, UC Min., 3 Aug., 2 Dec. 1837.

18 NLS, Lee papers, Ms 3442/fl54. A. Anderson to Principal Lee, St Andrews, 13 Feb. 1838.

19 Univ. St And. Libr., Spec. Coll., UC 400, UC Min., 3 Mar. 1838.

20 *NSA*, vol. ix, Fife and Kinross, parish of St Andrews, 471.

21 *Fifeshire Journal*, 25 Jan. 1838.

22 *Fife Herald*, 15 Mar. 1838.

23 *ibid.*, 9 Dec. 1845; *Fifeshire Journal*, 19 Apr. 1838, 2 Jan., 14 Dec. 1843, 11 Apr. 1844, 17 Apr., 15 May, 11 Dec. 1845.

24 *Fife Herald*, 19 Apr. 1838.

25 *Fifeshire Journal*, 8 Mar. 1838.

26 Perth Academy. xerox copy. A. Anderson to Andrew Anderson, jun., [son], Croft [Perth], 29 Aug. 1846.

27 *Perth Courier*, 23 July 1840, 11 Dec. 1845; *Perthshire Advertiser*, 10 Dec. 1846.

28 Information kindly supplied by Mrs K. Williams from the records of the British Association for the Advancement of Science.

29 Perth Academy. [A. Anderson to] Andrew Anderson, jun., [son], Hermitage, 13 Sep. 1844.

30 Univ. St And. Libr., Spec. Coll., MS36998/10. Same to same, Croft [Perth], 14 Oct. 1846.

31 Perth Academy. Xerox copy. Same to same, St Andrews, 24 Nov. 1844; Univ. St And. Libr., Spec. Coll., MS36998/9. Same to same, St Andrews, 18 May 1845.

32 Univ. St And. Libr., Spec. Coll., UC 400, UC Min., 25 Sep., 9 and 16 Dec. 1837, 25 Apr. 1839, 7 May, 22 Dec. 1842, 12 Jan., 30 June 1843, 24 Apr. 1846.

33 Commissioners for visiting the universities of Scotland, 1826-30, *Evidence, oral and documentary, vol. 3: University of St Andrews*, (London, 1837), [evidence of Dr T.Jackson], 129.

34 William Cochran, 'Sir David Brewster: an outline biography' in *'Martyr of Science': Sir David Brewster, 1781-1868: proceedings of a bicentenary symposium held at the Royal Scottish Museum on 21 November 1981*; ed. by A.D. Morrison-Low and J.R.R. Christie, (Edinburgh: Royal Scottish Museum, 1984), 13.

35 *Report [of the] St And[rews] Univ[ersity] Comm[issioners (Scotland)]*, (London: H.M.S.O., 1845), appendix no. II, [evidence of A. Anderson], 136.

36 *Fifeshire Journal*, 4 May 1843; *Perth Courier*, 4 May 1843.

37 Perth Academy. Xerox copy. A. Anderson to Andrew Anderson, jun., [son], St Andrews, 24 Nov. 1844; *Report St And. Univ. Comm.*, appendix no. II, [evidence of A. Anderson], 136.

38 eg. Univ. St And. Libr., Spec. Coll., UC 400, UC Min., 27 Jan., 1 Dec. 1838, 2 and 23 Feb., 31 May, 2 Nov. 1839, 1 and 15 Feb., 12 Dec. 1840, 6 Feb., 2 Dec. 1841, 10 Feb., 6 and 24 Mar., 15 Dec.1842.

39 Commissioners for visiting the universities of Scotland, 1826-30, *Evidence, oral and documentary, vol. 3: University of St Andrews*, [evidence of Dr T.Jackson], 140-1.

40 *NSA*, vol. ix, Fife and Kinross, parish of St Andrews, 491-2; R.G. Cant, *The University of St Andrews: a short history*, (Edinburgh: Scottish Academic Press, 1970), 106-9.

41 *ibid.*, 108 note; Univ. St And. Libr., Spec. Coll., UC 400, UC Min., 22 and 24 Nov. 1837, 3 Feb., 15 and 27 Dec. 1838, 5 Jan. 1839, 23 Sep. 1844.

42 Univ. St And. Libr., Spec. Coll., MS36998/9. A. Anderson to Andrew Anderson, jun., [son], St Andrews, 18 May 1845; *Fifeshire Journal*, 25 Apr. 1844.

43 Univ. St And. Libr., Spec. Coll., UC 400, UC Min., 17 Nov. 1838, 8 Apr. 1839

44 *Civil engineering: the university contribution;* ed. by Peter C.G. Isaac, (Newcastle-upon-Tyne: Oriel Press, 1970), 50-1; J. Coutts, *A history of the University of Glasgow from its foundation in 1451 to 1909,* (Glasgow: Maclehose, 1909), 390.

45 Univ. St And. Libr., Spec. Coll., UC 400, UC Min., 11 Sep. 1839; UY 452, St And. Sen. Min., 27 Mar. 1841.

46 Robert Anderson, 'Brewster and the reform of the Scottish universities' in *'Martyr of Science'*, 31-4; *Report St And. Univ. Comm.*, appendix no. II, [evidence of A. Anderson], 137.

47 M.M. Gordon, *The home life of Sir David Brewster, by his daughter, Mrs Gordon,* (Edinburgh: Edmonston & Douglas, 1870), 169, 426-7.

48 Univ. St And. Libr., Spec. Coll., UC Min., 1 Feb. 1840.

49 Univ. St And. Libr., Spec. Coll., UY 452, St And. Sen. Min., 5, 6, 7, 11 and 13 Mar. 1843.

50 Univ. St And. Libr., Spec. Coll., UC Min., 7 Nov. 1843; M.M.Gordon, *op. cit.*, 178-9.

51 Perth Academy. Xerox copy. A. Anderson to Andrew Anderson, jun., [son], St Andrews, 24 Nov. 1844.

52 *Report St And. Univ. Comm.*, appendix no. II, (evidence of Sir D. Brewster], 110.

53 Univ. St And. Libr., Spec. Coll., UC 400, UC Min., 22 and 25 Nov. 1842, 23 Feb., 2, 9 and 21 Mar. 1843; UY 452, St And. Sen. Min., 8 Mar. 1843; *Fifeshire Journal*, 16 and 30 Mar. 1843.

54 *ibid.*, 22 Dec. 1845; Univ. St And. Libr., Spec. Coll., Forbes papers, incoming correspondence 1846/7. Sir D. Brewster to J.D. Forbes, St Leonard's College, St Andrews, 20 Jan. 1846.

55 NLS, Lee papers, Ms 3445/ff177-82. William Spalding to Principal Lee, St Andrews, 29 Jan. 1846.

56   NLS, Lee papers, Ms 3445/f237. Same to same, [n.a.], 4[sic] Dec. 1846; Univ. St And. Libr., Spec. Coll., UY 452, St And. Sen. Min., 12 Dec. 1846; *Perth Courier*, 10 Dec. 1846.

EPILOGUE

On 15 December 1846, at 8am, nearly two hundred students, preceded by college professors and local dignitaries, escorted Adam Anderson's hearse from his lodgings to the outskirts of St Andrews. This followed the usual ceremony succeeding a professorial death. Six hours later the cortege arrived in Perth for a civic funeral. There all public bodies took part, including the council, presbytery, society of procurators, and water commissioners, as well as teachers and pupils from the public seminaries.[1] Anderson was interred in Greyfriars cemetery, overlooked by the water works.

Anderson was not forgotten immediately after the event. In April 1847, Perth Town Council accepted a gift of his portrait from J.M. Barclay, a local painter, to hang in the city halls.[2] Two years later, when a new philosophical and scientific institute was formed in Perth in reaction against the popularisation of the mechanics' institute, it was named the Andersonian Institution in his honour,[3] and as a symbol of a determination to return to truly educational objectives. Yet this new body and the memory both proved short-lived. In 1867 his grave remained unmarked until an obelisk was erected by public subscription.

On Anderson's death attempts were made to measure the man and his achievements. Early Victorian obituarists naturally laid stress on his personal qualities and piety, though also asserting that he had received inadequate recognition as a scientist. In particular, it was claimed that he had invented the Drummond and Bude lights before their accredited inventors. Certainly, in 1812, he had conducted experiments in which continuous streams of oxygen and hydrogen gases were thrown on a heated ball of carbonate of lime. The following year he had directed oxygen through the interior of the flame of an argand oil lamp.[4] In other words, Anderson (but probably others too) demonstrated the principles upon which the later inventions were based. Unlike Thomas Drummond, who worked for the Ordnance Survey, Anderson had no immediate practical application for the discovery. Significantly, far from making any personal claims to the invention, Anderson specifically referred to 'the Drummond light' in his private correspondence.[5] As a theoretical scientist nonetheless, his own originality was beyond dispute, even if his research yielded no great seminal work. In part this reflected the constraint of his responsibilities at Perth Academy, his genuine passion for teaching, and his total commitment to the communication of scientific knowledge to anyone who could be induced to listen. That priority survived his belated migration to an academic environment. Two further brakes on the depth of his pure research however, were the sheer breadth and diversity of his interests and his dedication to practical applications.

With contemporaries like Brewster and Forbes populating the field of Scottish physics in the early nineteenth century, relative distinction in pure science was elusive; as an applied scientist nonetheless, Anderson had a proven track record, which probably owed much, paradoxically, to his daily interaction in Perth with a wider society than he would have encountered in a more strictly academic environment. If his opportunities for demonstrating this capability were limited to the Perth area by the demands of his schoolteaching responsibilities, they still distinguished him from many strictly theoretical counterparts. His civil engineering achievements, particularly the provision of gas and water services, brought inestimable, long-term benefits to the population of Perth; the heart of his water system, for instance, remained operational until 1965. The city inherited too, as a by-product, one of Scotland's most impressive monuments of industrial archaeology. Other contributions were equally lasting. His consultancy in the navigational improvement of the Tay has tended to be overshadowed by the activities of professional engineers like the Stevensons. Yet his background presence as a source of dependable, impartial advice did much to fire the Perth council with the confidence to embark on such ambitious improvements. As a consequence, the continuing viability and prosperity of Perth as a port down to the present were assured. Likewise, the adoption of his solution to the problem of anchoring the east coast railway into the network centred on Perth spared the character and beauty of the town from suffering irreparable damage. It preserved the 'city feel', which owes much to the unspoilt, spacious surroundings of the Georgian terraces fronting the Inches. If these enduring triumphs were localised, as were those of many other early Victorian engineers, they were tangible and diverse.

Anderson reflected the social and political context of early nineteenth-century science, including its contradictions. He personified, for instance, the vitality of the contemporary provincial scene. It was possible to achieve distinction and success to a remarkable degree, while ignoring not only the centripetal attraction of London, but also the 'pull' of a nearby 'regional' scientific metropolis, Edinburgh. Such local and individual self-reliance, still possible in this period, underpinned the establishment of the British Association for the Advancement of Science as a provincial alternative to the metropolitan Royal Society. In Anderson's case, the same phenomenon could carry him direct from a provincial teaching post to the apex of science in Scotland, a university chair.

Clearly he also symbolised the enhanced significance of middle-class professionals in the reform era and, concurrently with his personal encyclopaedic interests, of their increasingly diverse specialisms. In his political sallies he underlined the concern of their liberal conservative wing to promote a variety of constitutional bulwarks against ultra-radicalism. The enthusiasm of his educational missions among artisans was coloured by anxiety to promote social sedation. Yet this talented polymath came from a background, which, though not impoverished, was likewise not wealthy. Was he then simply a clear-cut example of a 'marginal' man who employed science as a means of confirming his personal upward social mobility, whilst concurrently transmitting the values of an existing ruling class? Perhaps he was, but he also raised alternatives to them, however unintentionally, by widening horizons. He was concerned moreover with more than merely preserving the status quo, believing that its continuing validity depended on reforming its more flagrant abuses. Practical applications were not confined to science.

In another sense too his concern was wider than purely maintaining political or constitutional stability. He feared the entire challenge posed by science to religious belief. This was central to his role as an educationalist. Natural theology could, and he believed would, reconcile potential conflict between the claims of both. His life was dedicated to promoting cultural and social values, which promoted learning as a good in itself, not merely an aid to revelation of a Divine design. In his haste to modernise the curriculum of St Andrews, by introducing the 'mechanical arts which administer to the comforts and enjoyments of civilized life', he appears again a modernising force ahead of his time, a radical rather than a conservative. In the diversity of his interests and talents, he encapsulates the generalist ethos of the Scottish educational tradition at its best and most successful.

Like its creator, the water works continued to adapt to changing practical needs. Following the first refurbishment of 1972-74, the building served as Perth's tourist information centre for many years. It became redundant again in the 1990s, when the centre was transferred to a more central location. In 1992, the Round House acquired a new role, providing a permanent, dedicated art gallery for the extensive art collection of the celebrated Scottish Colourist artist, John Duncan Fergusson (1874-1961). This new function was temporarily suspended in 2003-05, when further conservation became necessary in the light of corrosion that was weakening the wrought iron structure of the dome. With £1 million provided by the Heritage Lottery Fund, Historic Scotland, and Perth & Kinross Council, a project lasting eighteenth months was initiated to dismantle the dome and rotunda; to clean, repair, and re-coat the 192 cast iron panels; to re-erect the whole; and to repair the stonework. Deploying as much original material as possible, in line with modern conservation principles, a specialist ironwork company, Casting Repairs of Chesterfield, undertook the task, with the entire project overseen by Allen, Gordon & Co., consulting civil and structural engineers of Perth. The project revealed the high quality work of the Dundee Foundry in the 1830s (previously highlighted by Anderson in his own report), as well as the original colour of the dome; that was then reinstated in the re-coating of the metal. Based too on original Anderson drawings, a new cast iron cap was designed for the top of the dome by John Sinclair, engineer of the project. This will allow air to flow through the dome, preventing fresh corrosion of the ironwork. Anderson's creation should therefore be safeguarded as a source of curiosity and admiration for future generations.[6]

NOTES

1   *Perth Courier*, 17 Dec. 1846; *Fife Herald*, 17 Dec. 1846.

2   PTC Min., 5 Apr. 1847. Barclay's painting, currently in Perth Museum and Art Gallery, was in fact copied from the original by Thomas Duncan RSA (1807-45), now in the possession of St Andrews University.

3   T.H. Marshall, *op. cit.*, 417.

4   *Perthshire Advertiser*, 10 Dec. 1846.

5   NCL, TCP, CHA4.288.40. A. Anderson to T Chalmers, Perth, 15 Oct. 1840.

6   http://www.antiques-scotland.co.uk/events/ fergusson_gallery_closure03.htm

GENERAL INDEX

The Abertay Historical Society

Honorary Presidents
Lord Provost of the City of Dundee
Principal of the University of Dundee
Principal of the University of St Andrews

President
Steve Connelly

Vice-President
Frances Grieve

General Secretary
Matthew Jarron
c/o University of Dundee Museum Services, Dundee DD1 4HN
e-mail: museum@dundee.ac.uk

Treasurer
Charlotte Lythe
90 Dundee Road, Broughty Ferry, Dundee DD5 1DW
e-mail: c.lythe1@btinternet.com

Book Editors
Dr W Kenefick & Dr A MacDonald
Department of History, University of Dundee, Dundee DD1 4HN

Sales Secretary
Catherine Smith
SUAT, 55 South Methven Street, Perth PH1 5NX
e-mail: csmith@suat.co.uk

The Society was founded in May 1947 and exists to promote interest in local history. For further information, please visit our website at www.abertay.org.uk

Publications of the Abertay Historical Society currently in print

No. 28   Enid Gauldie, *One Artful and Ambitious Individual, Alexander Riddoch (1745-1822), (Provost of Dundee 1787-1819).* (1989) ISBN 0 900019 24 7

No. 34   Ian McCraw, *The Fairs of Dundee.* (1994) ISBN 0 90019 30 1

No. 35   Annette M. Smith, *The Nine Trades of Dundee.* (1995) ISBN 0 900019 31 X

No. 37   Michael St John, *The Demands of the People, Dundee Radicalism 1850-1870.* (1997) ISBN 0 900019 33 6

No. 38   W.M. Mathew, *Keiller's of Dundee, The Rise of the Marmalade Dynasty 1800-1879.* (1998) ISBN 0 900019 35 2

No. 39   Lorraine Walsh, *Patrons, Poverty & profit: Organised Charity in Nineteenth Century Dundee.* (2000) ISBN 0 900019 35 2

No. 40   Stewart Howe, *William Low & Co., A Family Business History.* (2000) ISBN 0 900019 36 0

No. 41   Ian McCraw, *Victorian Dundee at Worship.* (2002) ISBN 0 900019 37 9

No. 42   Andrew Murray Scott, *Dundee's Literary Lives vol 1: Fifteenth to Nineteenth Century.* (2003) ISBN 0 900019 38 7

No. 43   Andrew Murray Scott, *Dundee's Literary Lives vol 2: Twentieth Century.* (2004) ISBN 0 900019 39 5

No. 44   Claire Swan, *Scottish Cowboys and the Dundee Investors.* (2004) ISBN 0 900019 40 9

No. 45   Annette M. Smith, *The Guildry of Dundee: A History of the Merchant Guild of Dundee up to the 19th century.* (2005) ISBN 0 900019 42 5

No. 46   Mary Verschuur, *A Noble and Potent Lady: Katherine Campbell, Countess of Crawford.* (2006) ISBN 0 900019 43 3

All publications may be obtained through booksellers or by post from the Hon Sales Secretary, Abertay Historical Society, SUAT, 55 South Methven Street, Perth, PH1 5NX (e-mail: csmith@suat.co.uk)